Bittersweet Blessing

MTV 16 and Pregnant

By Ashley Salazar

MTV PRESS

FIRST PUBLISHED IN THE UNITED STATES OF AMERICAN IN 2012 BY:
MTV Press
1515 Broadway
New York, NY 10036
mtv.com

DISTRIBUTED BY
powerHouse Books
37 Main Street, Brooklyn, NY 11201
PHONE 212 604 9074 FAX 212 366 5247
powerHouseBooks.com

Lyrics to "Find My Way Home" and "Beautiful Girl" used
with permission of William Fitzsimmons

Design by Susan Choi

FIRST EDITION
2012 / 10 9 8 7 6 5 4 3 2 1

PRINTED AND BOUND IN THE UNITED STATES OF AMERICA

ISBN: 978-1576875841

For Callie
my angel, my miracle, my complete motivation,
and the reason for where I am today.

GETTING STARTED

I used to keep a little blog on Myspace. It basically consisted of random thoughts on anything and everything that popped into my head. I guess it was a way for me to deal with all the craziness that was going on in my life at that point.

Then my aunt Jen, who is an avid blog reader, encouraged me to create a more organized blog to talk about everything I was going through and that I was willing to share. I decided to do it because I thought maybe it could help whomever was reading it to know what the experience of being a pregnant teen was really like.

I got pregnant in April of my junior year. I was seventeen and it was not how I pictured spending the summer before my senior year. It changed my life forever and forced me to make a lot of difficult decisions.

It pushed me to finish high school early and take college classes, which I had wanted to do but had never gotten around to. It made me realize that I wanted to get an education. I didn't want to be working a boring, all-day job that I hated, making little-to-no money. So, in that way, my situation was good: it pushed me to better myself. But I also had to make sacrifices that I will have to live with for the rest of my life.

Soon after I found out I was pregnant, I was chosen to be filmed for an episode of MTV's *16 and Pregnant*. Because of my blog and the show, my life has been an open book for anyone to judge or to learn from. I've had to make some very painful choices, and by sharing my experiences I hope that I can help young girls who are going through what I did to know that they are not alone.

Okay, here goes...

June

FINDING OUT

Let's think back: the day I found out was crazy. I must have already been at least a month along. I think I didn't really want to face the truth, even though deep down I knew something wasn't right. I had googled the symptoms of pregnancy and I had most of them. Period symptoms can be similar to pregnancy symptoms, so I kept hoping I was just late. I was so frightened and confused. I desperately wanted to talk to someone, but I avoided dealing with it as long as possible because it meant facing the reality that I was pregnant and telling my family.

In the end, it was my mom who confronted me about it because she suspected something was going on. She had noticed that I was more exhausted than usual and was having major mood swings. She called me from work and said, "Ashley, is there something that you need to tell me?"

I told her I had missed my period. Even though we argue and things haven't always been easy for us, my mom and I are close and I can talk to her about anything. That night, she brought home a pregnancy test for me.

It was one of those digital ones that flash when the result is in. She handed it to me and I went into the bathroom, still praying it would all just go away. I remember I didn't want to miss the stick so I peed in a cup and dipped it in. Then I put the test on the ledge of the tub and sat down on the floor with my arms wrapped around my legs. I think my mind was mostly blank. I just remember thinking, *Please be negative, please be negative...*over and over.

I couldn't move. I was too terrified. Finally my mom knocked on the door and I let her in. She pointed to the stick and said, "Ashley, you're pregnant." I was overwhelmed with anger and frustration. I snapped, "Mom, stop being so negative!" "Look," she said, pointing again at the stick. Then she walked out. It's kind of a blur now, but I will never forget the look on her face as she left me alone to think about what had really just happened. Like me, she was terrified and overwhelmed. She got pregnant with me when she was a teenager, so I knew this brought up a lot of issues for her. She knows from experience how hard it is to raise a child on your own, before you've had a chance to live your own life. The last thing she ever wanted was for me to have to go through what she did at such a young age.

My mom did remarry when I was very young and had another child, my little sister Mia. I consider my stepfather, Gilbert, to be my real father. I have always called him dad and only think of my biological father as just that—a biological parent. In fact, my earliest memories of my stepfather are of me being mad at their wedding because it was no longer going to be just me and my mom. They're divorced now, but my he's still a huge part of my life.

After my mom left, I felt the floor disappear under my feet. I was pregnant. It was too huge to take in. I couldn't even understand what it all meant at that moment. I just wanted to pretend it wasn't happening. My mom wouldn't let me. I went to my room, curled up in my bed and let the tears roll down my face. A few minutes later, she came in asking, "What are you going to do now?"

Good question. My first instinct was to do nothing, but that wasn't going to work. Pregnancies don't just go away if you ignore them, do they?

TELLING THE FATHER

Even though I had dreaded knowing for sure, it was a relief to not have this huge awful secret anymore. But before I could wrap my head around what it all meant, my mom was insisting I deal with the next hard thing: telling the father.

I was terrified to do this. The last thing any eighteen-year-old guy wants to hear is, "Hey, I'm pregnant and the baby's yours." The worst part was, we weren't even dating anymore. Justin had broken up with me over a month earlier and I had never really gotten over him. We weren't even together when the baby was conceived. It was one of those things that just kind of happens after you break up, but leaves you feeling even worse.

I wanted to put off telling Justin as long as possible. I didn't even know what I was going to say. But my mom insisted I call him right away. So that night, after I took the test, I picked up my cell phone and called Justin. It was the hardest phone call I have ever had to make.

His reaction was not what I had expected. I was shocked by how supportive he seemed. He promised me that everything would be okay, that we would figure it out together. He was working at Taco Bell and couldn't leave his shift, so we agreed to meet the next day. But when I saw him the next morning, it felt like the sweet supportive Justin was gone. We met up on the bus and sat in silence the whole way to school. I think we were both too shocked to say anything.

I kept thinking about the first time we spoke to one another. I had noticed him around school and thought he had the most beautiful eyes I had ever seen. They had a way of making him look sad and mischievous at the same time. Then one day we ended up on the bus together coming home from school. I was chewing gum and looking out the window with my headphones on, so I hadn't really noticed anyone else on the bus.

I felt a tap on my shoulder and turned around to see those eyes looking down at me. He asked me for a piece of gum. Normally, I hate giving out gum (once you give out one piece, everyone starts asking and you end up with an empty pack). I usually say that I'm chewing my last piece. But he was so cute, I couldn't say no. I gave him a piece and we chatted for a while. When he got off at the stop before mine, I realized that he lived three blocks away from me. Funny, huh? The boy next door.

Now here we were, on the bus right back where we started. Except this time he wasn't asking for gum. He wasn't saying anything at all. I guess neither of us knew what to say. He offered to find a way to help me pay for an abortion. I guess it hadn't really sunk in for him yet that I was more leaning towards going through with the pregnancy. Later, I heard he was going around accusing me of either lying about being pregnant or getting pregnant on purpose.

Neither of which was true, of course. I think he was so freaked out that it was easier to be angry at me than to really deal with what was happening.

Really, I thought he seemed as clueless as I was. And I was pretty clueless. I was seventeen. It was the first day of knowing I was pregnant. It hadn't settled in and I was so confused. I think he could tell how much I wanted him to be the "supportive boyfriend" and that pressure probably freaked him out. At the time, it seemed like it would be less scary if we went through it together. I'm sure that seemed strange to him though, since we weren't together anymore. I just couldn't understand how he could be so quiet and cold when it was clear that I needed warmth and support. I guess it was a true test that we weren't really in love and deep down I knew it.

That was the beginning of a very bad period for us. At the time I was extremely angry at him for the things he was saying and for not being supportive. Now I know that he was just as scared and confused as I was. We all say and do things that we aren't proud of or later regret. I get that—now.

JUSTIN

I guess I should go back and explain a little bit about Justin and our relationship. If we had never started dating, my life would be very different now. When I think back on how we met, it seems crazy that it ended up with us creating a baby. If you had told me when I first met him that things were going to end up the way they did, I would never have believed it.

I first saw Justin my sophomore year across the cafeteria at our school, Prosper High. He was a year ahead of me, so he must have been a junior. I remember thinking how cute he was, but then I didn't see him around much. He was friends with the older sister of a friend of mine and through her I found out that he had recently moved to Texas from California.

One night later that year, I was at my friend's house and Justin showed up with her older sister's boyfriend. We were dying my friend's hair, so I was wearing a grubby T-shirt and *Family Guy* boxers. He was the last person I ever expected to walk in. I felt shy and embarrassed, but he definitely didn't notice what I was wearing. When I asked him about it later, he barely remembered that day, never mind the *Family Guy* boxers. Guys are like that, I guess.

In my junior year, we ended up in a second semester speech class together. He was quiet and usually fell asleep in class. Or he would spend his time drawing and doodling. Justin's an amazing artist. He does these really cool graffiti drawings and kids were always asking him to draw something for them. I really wanted him to do one for me, too, but I was always too shy to ask.

Then one day I ran into him in my neighborhood. I had just gotten hair extensions and I had on jeans, a graphic T-shirt, and a gray cardigan—no *Family Guy* boxers this time. I was about to walk past him when he said hi to me. I had my headphones on again, so at first I thought he was some weirdo and I almost kept walking. When I realized he was the cute guy from school, I must have blushed so badly. He told me he was on his way to Walmart and we exchanged numbers.

After that we started texting each other every day. At first it wasn't flirty, just a lot of talking. But I liked him a lot. I was pretty sure he liked me too, so I didn't get why he wasn't making a move.

Then he told a friend of mine that he didn't want to get involved with anyone because he wanted to move back to California.

He had moved to McKinney with his mom, stepfather and two younger brothers and was super homesick for California. We had very similar experiences growing up. Both of us were raised by a stepfather whom we considered to be our real dad, and neither of us really knew our biological fathers. I think that made us feel close because we both understood where the other was coming from without having to explain. In the end, even though he tried to avoid it, we ended up getting involved anyway. He even came over and met my family. He was very polite—even my mom said so.

At first, before we became "official," he made a big thing about keeping the fact that we were seeing each other private, because we weren't actually dating. But, little by little, he relaxed and started holding my hand in the hallway and kissing me before class. Then one day we were hanging out at my house and he said, "Okay I want to give us a try."

It's funny, writing about it here, I remember all the great things about when we were together and

then I start to wonder why we broke up. But at the time it made sense. We kind of ran out of things to talk about. Finally, one morning I just asked him, "Is this even working?" and he said, "No." That was it. He broke up with me right before first period, in the hallway at school. I was devastated. I remember I went to psych class and cried all through it.

Looking back, it's hard to believe that we were together only two months. Now we'll be connected for the rest of our lives.

PHYSICAL FITNESS DAY

Most people, when they break up, try to avoid each other. That wasn't the case with Justin and me. After he broke up with me, we did our own thing for a while, but still talked and texted on and off. He seemed to still want to spend time with me (or maybe I just wanted to believe that he did), and I wasn't really over him. Looking back, I can see that I should have stayed away—being "just friends" was emotionally confusing for me—but at the time I thought I could handle it.

We would sometimes hang out in the mornings, either on the bus or in the cafeteria where all the students would gather to wait for the school bell to ring. Mostly we would talk about random stuff, as we had stopped having things to talk about by then. Then, one night, we sort of joked that maybe we would "meet up" the following morning. I knew that we were really making a plan to have sex, but I convinced myself that I was okay with that.

Even now, I have no clear answer for why I would agree to have sex with someone who had already broken my heart. In all honesty, sometimes I just don't think things through properly. Sometimes, in my head, I make myself think what I want to believe. I was infatuated with Justin and there was probably a part of me that thought maybe we would get back together. It seems desperate and sad, but that's the frame of mind I was in at the time.

The next day was April 1st of 2009—physical fitness day at school. Physical fitness day is that awful day where the state tests you on how physically fit you are by making you do exercises and stretches. Then, at the end of all the exercises, you have to run a mile in under twelve minutes. My friends and I would always lie about how many push-ups or crunches we did, so we could breeze through the day.

That morning I drove to school in my new blue Chevy Cobalt. I got my driver's license later than most of my friends, so I had only just started being able to drive. Justin had wanted a ride to school, but I couldn't give him one because I wasn't insured and my mom wouldn't let me take anyone in the car with me, so we agreed to meet at school.

When I got to the school parking lot, I waited for Justin in my car. I saw him get off the bus, and I sent him a text message telling him where I was. We knew we didn't have much time before the bell rang, so he got in the car and we talked a little, but not much. We drove off and things escalated quickly from there. We didn't even fool around much. We just sort of did it and that was that.

We did not discuss protection. Not because we were in the heat of the moment, because we weren't. We were just stupid and careless. I guess he assumed that I was on the pill, or just didn't care otherwise. I had been taught that the most effective way to prevent an unwanted pregnancy is by being on birth control and using a second method, such as a condom. So the thought of using protection did run through my head. Unfotunatley, I chose to ignore/forget everything I had learned. When I was younger and my mother explained to me what a condom was and what it was used for, I remember feeling disgusted and embarrassed. I wish now I had taken her more seriously.

The thought of STDs never entered my mind, which it should have. I knew he had been with other girls, but didn't consider the fact that I was potentially putting myself at risk by not using a condom. Foolishly, I only thought of other girls out of jealously or insecurity.

He didn't force me. I had enough time to think it through and I decided, *What the heck? How could this hurt me?* I even remember that before we had sex, we asked each other, "Do we really want to do this?" He made it clear to me that we would not get back together. Of course, I felt bad, but not bad enough to stop me from going through with it.

Maybe I went through with it out of a sense of unfinished business. We had sex once before, at my house, but it hadn't gone well. Maybe, subconsciously, we both felt we needed to prove we could do it "right." We didn't use protection that time, either. It lasted only a couple of seconds. At the time, I mostly believed that two seconds, or even five minutes, wouldn't lead to pregnancy—as long as he didn't "finish." While I didn't get pregnant that time, I certainly learned from the next time how wrong I was to believe that.

The time at my house didn't bother me, since we were still going out then. But, after that morning in my car, I felt hurt. Hurt and confused about what had happened. Honestly, the sex was not very enjoyable, no offense to Justin. I wasn't sexually active and, because of that, it hurt and I was sore. It was one of those moments that leaves you feeling bad about yourself and wondering why you would make such a foolish decision to do something so huge with such a lack of passion and love.

Occasionally, lying in bed at night, I get kind of haunted by that day. I sometimes have mental pictures of things that I do not want to see and things that I can't get rid of. I think of all the who's, the where's, the what's, the how's, and, most importantly, the why's

Why would I do something that was so demeaning and careless to myself? Did I have such little self-respect?

I just never imagined what the outcome of that morning could possibly have been. Actually, make that outcomes. Plural. My actions that morning started a chain of events that changed my life, and the lives of those closest to me, forever.

THE HARDEST DECISION EVER

Once I had told Justin and my immediate family, I had to decide just what I was going to do next. There were really only three options: abortion, adoption, or teen motherhood. I know a lot of people will judge me for even considering abortion, but when you aren't prepared, when it's a mistake and you aren't in love with the father (or he isn't in love with you), every option runs through your mind. Deep down, though, I knew that I could never go through with an abortion. It just wasn't the right choice for me.

That left me with what seems like one of the hardest choices anyone could ever have to make: adoption or motherhood. The more the reality of being pregnant settled in, the more I began to question if I was capable of taking care of a baby. I could hardly take care of myself. My baby wouldn't have a father at home, and I definitely did not want a father I thought was going to be in and out of my baby's life. That's how I felt about my biological father and I swore that I would never repeat what I consider to be my parents' mistakes. I did not want my baby going through some of the things I experienced in my childhood.

Another thing was my emotional state. Was I ready to take on this stressful challenge? Was I willing to not be able to participate in family vacations or to miss out on going out with friends? I didn't know yet. I hoped so, because I was already feeling attached to this baby. But then it wasn't about me or what I wanted, it was about what would be best for the baby.

I told my mom I was considering adoption and she was very supportive. She was only nineteen when she had me and raised me pretty much on her own. She knew what I would be up against if I chose to raise a baby on my own. In fact, I think she might have been even more afraid for me than I was for myself.

She was also worried about what it would mean for her. She raised me without my biological father, but she had a lot of help from my grandparents because we lived near them in Harlingen, Texas when I was small. That caused a lot of conflict in the family. I thought of my grandparents, Mimi and Papa, as my parents as well. They are my legal guardians and I am very close to them.

They had a lot of input in the way my mom raised me, and I did not want to have to deal with my mom's influence in every parenting decision that I made, the way she'd had to. I think she was worried that she wouldn't be able to help me as much as my grandparents helped her. She has a demanding job and works long hours. She was afraid it would be impossible for me to take care of a baby without a lot of help, because she knew how hard it had been for her even with help. But she also knew how difficult it would be to go through with adoption.

I tried to be confident about adoption, but looking back I remember my mother's exact words when she asked if I was sure. She warned me that it would be the hardest decision I would ever have to make. "Okay, Ashley," she said, "I'll ask you again in a few months when the baby starts kicking." I remember thinking, "I'm so set on adoption, I could never get attached." Wrong. Just three short months later, without even having a first noticeable kick, I can't count how many times I cried and cried over the thought of going through with the adoption.

It is, in fact, the hardest decision. Mother is always right. The doctor's appointments, ultrasound, hearing the baby's heartbeat, and seeing it move and grow made it that much more complicated.

BEING PREGNANT

Meanwhile, I tried to focus on the positives, even though I knew I had a painful choice ahead of me. Being pregnant was an amazing experience and the changes to my body were crazy: seeing myself grow and knowing that I was nurturing and growing another life. I was lucky because I didn't have much morning sickness. I did have a lot of back pain, though—nothing like a big belly sticking out in front to strain your back.

I had to completely change my diet. I had always lived on tea, but now I couldn't have caffeine. I never used to eat breakfast, but now I woke up nauseous and had to eat right away. It was like that all day. If I was hungry I had to eat right away or I would feel sick to my stomach. Once I got in trouble for eating goldfish in art class. My teacher gave me detention even though I tried to explain that I had to eat because I was pregnant.

My food cravings were odd and kind of interesting. I had always loved bacon, but now I couldn't stand the smell of it. Or onions. Anything with onions made me sick. I loved tuna, but had to limit how much of it I ate because of the mercury. I couldn't have Caesar dressing, hot dogs, and a lot of other random foods that I loved and ate all the time.

Sweets didn't appeal that much, so that was good. The thought of Chipotle, a taco restaurant, made me want to throw up. One of the weirdest things was my strawberry cravings: strawberry milk, strawberry shortcake, strawberry yogurt, strawberry shakes, strawberry ice cream, and fresh strawberries. Anything with strawberries was wonderful. One time, before I knew I was pregnant, I made my Mimi (my maternal grandmother) drive in a thunderstorm to Steak 'N' Shake to get me a strawberry milkshake at 10 o'clock at night.

Some of the bad side effects: heartburn and getting muscle cramps out of the blue. Oh, and no matter how hard I tried, I would fall asleep once a day for a minimum of an hour and a half. I could have been studying or doing something productive instead. Then, to top it off, I couldn't sleep at night. I was always thirsty, too. I remember waking up in the middle of the night (every night) and trudging downstairs to chug a whole bottle of water.

I only gained twelve pounds at first, but by the end I had gained thirty. I could literally feel my body stretching every day. I hated gaining weight and not being able to wear any of my favorite clothes anymore. But I still never really wore maternity clothes. I did try to go clothes shopping in the maternity section once by myself and once with my mom, but they were both pretty awful experiences. So my wardrobe for the entire pregnancy consisted of shorts that I accidentally bought too big a few months before I got pregnant, sweats, stretchy tank tops and loose t-shirts. Pretty good looking, huh?

The other sucky thing was that my hair got thicker. I've heard lots of women love that about being pregnant, but I hated it. I had always had my hair thinned because it was too thick to begin with. Now it was just crazy. I even had to take out my hair extensions, and anyone who knows me knows how much I love my extensions.

Overall, though, aside from the cramps, heartburn, and physical exhaustion, it was a relatively easy pregnancy.

NOT LIKE TV AT ALL

The Secret Life of the American Teenager—I used to love to watch that show on ABC Family. But now I feel like it glamorizes teenage pregnancy. Pregnancy is not all great and easy. You don't simply get all the help in the world. Not even *16 and Pregnant* shows every bad thing about teenage pregnancy. It's a lot closer to reality, but the producers can only fit so much into a one hour episode.

They don't show what goes on in a teen's mind that makes them end up in that situation in the first place. Like how you think, *If I'm smart, if we do it the right way, if we don't do it for very long, nothing will happen.* That's wrong. The only way to avoid getting pregnant is to use protection or, better yet, to abstain from having sex at all. A lot of girls think, *He told me he loves me, so no matter what happens we will always be together*. The reality is, no matter how much two people love each other, having a baby before you've finished high school will take the romance out of any relationship.

Sex may seem like a good idea at the time, but it's not. Chances are your boyfriend doesn't really love you. Even if you both think you are in love, the relationship most likely won't last beyond high school. It might, but that's a rare thing.

It seems like so often on these shows the father magically comes back into the baby's life, at least in the beginning. In reality most teen girls who get pregnant won't have any help from the father. Or the grandparents do almost everything for the baby. Or the friends of the pregnant teen organize a way for her to continue in school, get her a job, and offer their unconditional support. But really, how many teenagers are willing to sacrifice their lives for somebody else's baby?

Do these shows really portray every horrible detail of what she had to go through? Do they show her missing out on everything because of her baby? Do they show the ridicule she had to endure? Do they show the stares of the people she passes in public or the judgmental looks she gets as the pregnant teenager in the obstetrician's office? I don't think so.

That's a big part of why I wanted to do *16 and Pregnant*. I thought I could help other girls like me who don't have help. I wanted to warn them about what they will have to go through so they don't make the same mistake I made. Truthfully, I was in a much better position than a lot of other pregnant teens. I was a senior and was able to graduate early. A lot of girls get pregnant even younger than I was and have to deal with high school and a baby.

Pregnancy as a teenager is draining physically and emotionally. Having to decide whether or not to give up something that is part of you is unimaginably painful.

Then there's the stuff you have to miss out on because you are pregnant. Like when my whole family talked about doing something I couldn't; Hurricane Harbor, Six Flags, vacations. The only place I had ever wanted to go was the Northeast, mostly New York. My mom took my younger sister to Philadelphia, New York, and New Jersey. They invited me and asked if I could skip school. I desperately wanted to go, but I had a presentation and material to go over during the days that I would have missed. It might not seem like that big of a deal, but it felt awful knowing I couldn't go because of my carelessness. I most likely wouldn't have been in those classes if I hadn't needed to get my education finished fast.

Teenage pregnancy is not glamorous. You may love your baby, but it isn't fun. It isn't a party. Buying baby clothes, accessories, and baby showers are not quite at the top of your "To Do" list. Taking vitamins, going to doctor's appointments, eating right, finishing school, getting a job, earning money to support yourself and your baby; those are your priorities.

It's not like TV at all. Take it from somebody who knows.

ALL THE JUDGING AND STARING

Once the reality began to set in and the shocked, numb feeling went away, I started to feel mad about everything. Actually, more sad, which is probably why I cried all the time. I didn't know what I was feeling. It was all mixed up. I regretted getting myself into this mess. Even check-ups with the doctor made me sad.

I remember one time sitting in the waiting room and this girl walked out of the exam room with her mother. She was definitely a year or two younger than me and she still looked really small, stomach-wise. I thought, *Okay, maybe it's her mom that's pregnant*. Then I saw the gauze with a Band-Aid on her arm, showing that she had gotten blood work done, which you usually do at your first visit. She did not look happy at all. If it was her first visit to the gynecologist she probably didn't know what to expect. Her mom didn't even seem to acknowledge her.

To make it worse, people were staring at her. I wanted to tell them to mind their own business, because I knew how it felt to have people staring at you like that. It's awful to have people looking at you, wondering what a girl so young is doing there. *Well, it's quite obvious, lady!* I felt like I could relate to how she might have felt.

Maybe she wasn't sad and her mom wasn't upset. Maybe I was reading the signs all wrong. Maybe. It just made me remember my first visit after I found out I was pregnant. I didn't know what to expect at all. I was so intimidated and frightened. Seeing the baby and hearing the heartbeat made it all so real. Not to mention the disturbing type of ultrasound I got the first time. I won't go into detail, but let me just say that when the doctor pulled the wand out, I remember thinking, "Please, let that be for my stomach."

In truth, I didn't know what that girl was thinking or feeling, but I really don't see how someone that young could not be upset or scared or sad about being pregnant. I basically just felt for her. It made me sad, but it also made me feel not so alone.

DOING IT ALONE

I feel so different from other girls I've seen on teen pregnancy shows. The majority of these girls have the babies' father supporting them, at least in the beginning. I was completely alone.

I believe that the only support I ever had from Justin was for the decision to pursue adoption because he wasn't ready to be a father. I'm not trying to trash or belittle him. Of course, a baby is the farthest thing from the mind of an eighteen-year-old boy. I just felt let down that he wasn't more supportive in the beginning.

I wasn't ready either. I wasn't prepared to have to make such painful decisions on my own. I would have loved support, but having to do it all on my own has made me a stronger person.

QUESTIONS AND CONCERNS

I remember watching the season finale of *16 and Pregnant*. It was such an emotional episode. It was about a teen couple, Catelynn and Tyler, who chose adoption for their baby. I have never cried that hard at anything in my life. It was a definite eye opener for me. It triggered so many emotions and forced me to face so many difficult questions.

What would it be like when I actually had to go through the process of adoption? Would I be able to put aside what I was feeling and focus on what was right for my baby? I couldn't imagine the feeling of seeing my baby and then having to hand it over to its adoptive parents. Maybe not even getting to hold it.

Deep down though, I knew no matter how painful it was going to be, it really all came down to what would be best for this baby. I couldn't provide my baby with the life it deserved. Not like financially stable adults in a strong marriage could; a family that couldn't have children, a family with a stay-at-home mother and a caring father. Adoption might be the best gift I could give my baby, no matter how much it was going to hurt.

But I also had major doubts. A huge part of me wanted to keep my baby. What if I chose a couple and went through the whole adoption process, but then decided to keep my baby? What happens in these adoptions if the mother to decides to keep it? I would feel awful, but a big part of me felt like I wasn't as strong as Catelynn. At least, I wasn't yet.

A DECISION

The worst part of being pregnant was just how awful and guilty I felt all the time. I would feel the baby kicking; so innocent, happy, healthy and content in the safety of its mommy, totally unaware that I was considering adoption. I kept going over the same arguments. It will be happier if I give it up because I won't be able to spoil it. I won't be able to devote twenty-four hours of my time to being a mother. It would have a struggling single mom and it wouldn't have a daddy.

I wanted so badly to keep my baby, but I couldn't come up with a single argument to support that decision. Would it be better for my baby to be raised by an unemployed, single teenager who barely knew how to fold laundry or make mac and cheese? Or by a loving adult couple who were in a position to provide a stable home life?

The right choice seemed obvious. I had to be honest with myself that the real reason I didn't want to go through with adoption was that I knew it was going to hurt too much (which is more about what I needed than about what would be best for my baby).

I just wanted my baby to have a better family life than I did. Not that I had it all that bad, but I didn't have a stay-at-home mom and, even though my stepdad has always been a true father to me, I know how it is to feel like your biological father doesn't care. No matter how strong a person is, you never hear anyone who grew up without two stable and loving parents say that they didn't feel like something was missing. If I chose adoption my baby would have plenty of attention. If I kept it, I wouldn't be around enough because of work and college. My mom would be working all the time so she wasn't in a position to step in and help me take care of it. It would grow up knowing a nanny and day cares, not its family.

So, even though it wasn't what I really wanted, I came to the conclusion that adoption was the right path for me and my baby. It was a painful choice, but I was seventeen and I could barely take care of myself. I wasn't ready to take on the responsibility of being a parent. I hadn't looked into day cares or anything else that a baby needs. I didn't even know what else a baby needed. I already loved this baby so much I didn't know how I was going to ever give it up, but I hoped it would thank me later.

Even though my decision was made, it didn't make things easier. I just tried to be as strong as I could and focus on finishing school, or my mom wouldn't help me with anything, baby or no baby.

Later, when I'm done with my education and I am ready to start a family, maybe all this will have been worth it. Then I will be able to give a baby a happy life and spoil it with everything it could ever want or need. It will have a stay-at-home mom and a loving daddy. That's all I want: for my baby to have two loving and devoted parents.

16 AND PREGNANT

After I made my decision, I kept thinking about Catelynn and Tyler from the first season of *16 and Pregnant* and how strong they were. I would go to the show's site a lot to see what people were saying about their decision to go through with adoption. I thought maybe the positive comments Catelynn and Tyler got would help me feel better about what I was doing.

Then someone told me on Myspace that MTV was casting for a new season. I thought, *Why not apply?* I sent in my name, a recent photo of myself, a description of my situation, and a link to my blog.

The next day, I received an email with a long questionnaire from the MTV people. I filled it out and returned it right away. I didn't know what my family would think if I got picked, but I figured I would cross that bridge when I came to it.

A few days later, the casting department called me. They asked a lot of questions about my situation and what I was going to do. I don't remember exactly what was said, but it was a long conversation. They wanted lots of details. They gave me an assignment to make a video about my everyday life. It wasn't easy. If you've ever been on camera or tried to film yourself acting natural, you'll know what I mean.

Before I went any further I talked it over with my mom to make sure I had her permission. At first she was nervous about me appearing on television, but then she decided that it might help me to deal better with the pregnancy and the adoption. I think at that point she was so worried about me she was willing to try anything if it would keep me from crying all the time.

I guess my video was good enough, because a couple of weeks later I got a call saying they were going to cast me. I couldn't believe it! I was so excited. It gave me something to focus on other than pregnancy and adoption. It was at this point that my mom started feeling more nervous. I don't think she thought I'd actually get picked. When I did she felt like I had tried this hard, how could she not let me do it? I was excited, though, because I thought that being filmed and being on the show would help me stick to my adoption decision and deal with the whole thing in a better way.

August

FILMING

In August, MTV's production crew (two camera people, a sound person, a director, and a few others) arrived to begin filming. Most were from New York or Los Angeles, though one of the crew members was a local from Texas. At first they would show up at the house a couple of times a week. Towards the end of my pregnancy they were with me almost every day.

At first it was strange, having a camera crew following me around and filming everything I did. I was self-conscious about my hair, my makeup, and how I looked in general—already an issue when you're pregnant. I'm sure I was so awkward in the beginning that they had to throw out the first few days of footage. Then, more quickly than you might think, I forgot they were there and went about my life. When I look at scenes from my episode now, they seem so natural that I have to really think about where the crew was when they were filming.

Not everyone around me was happy about the filming or wanted to be on the show, which I totally respected. The crew was amazing at working around those people and not capturing them on film. Now that I've seen my episode, it's actually pretty impressive how they were able to do that so well.

GOING THROUGH WITH IT

Once I had made my decision, I met with a caseworker, Ashley, from an adoption agency called Gladney Center for Adoption. She came out to my house and met with me and my mom. We discussed picking the adoptive family and going through the adoptive process. It was her job to prepare me for the day when I would hand my baby over to its new parents.

Meeting with Ashley was totally overwhelming because it made the whole thing so real. I always knew it was going to be hard, but she really brought it home for me. I felt tears coming the whole time we talked, but I held it in because this is where I knew I had to be strong.

She talked about how hard it would be to carry the baby for nine months and love it and then deliver and go home without it. She reassured me that my doubts were normal and told me that she had never met a birth mother who didn't wish that she could parent her baby if her circumstances were different. I had so many questions. I wasn't even sure where to begin. I guess my biggest fear was not picking the right couple.

Ashley was really nice, but it was a very emotional experience because I still couldn't believe I was actually going through with adoption. Now it was official. There was no turning back. It was her job as a counselor to help me work through all this, but I knew I would never truly be at peace with the decision. How could I be?

IT'S A GIRL

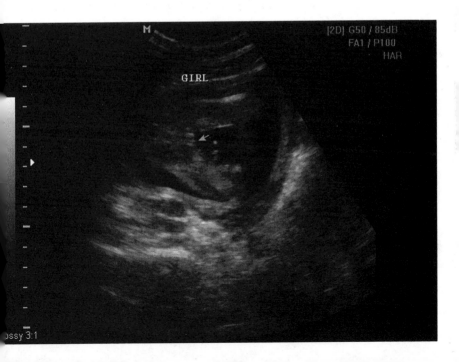

Even though I wasn't supposed to be getting attached, I decided to find out the sex of the baby. I wanted to know. This baby had become everything.

On the same day I met Ashley, I also had a doctor's appointment for my twenty-week sonogram. My head was still spinning from that meeting. Now I was about to have the first real look at the life growing inside me that I had just been talking about giving up.

First, I found out that I hadn't even gained ten pounds by my fifth month. I'd gained more like five or six. That was with my clothes and shoes on. I kind of worried about it, but I wasn't complaining.

The best part was that I found out I was having a girl! I couldn't help thinking how cute she was going to be. I imagined her with my brown hair and Justin's amazing eyes. I also got to see and hear her little heartbeat again. I even saw the four chambers of the heart, her spine, her little bones, and her feet and hands.

I couldn't believe there was a living thing inside me. Up to that point the baby had been an *it*. Now my baby was a *she* and the love I felt for her practically made my heart burst open. It was one thing to think about it, but actually seeing her was amazing and made her so real to me. Even though knowing the sex definitely made me feel more attached, it didn't change the arguments going on in my head. It just made everything that much more intense. More than ever I wanted to make the best possible decision for her.

There was one scary thing though. The doctor explained to me that at the moment the baby was breech, meaning her head was positioned up instead of down. This can cause complications during birth. She explained that this was fairly normal and even common at this point in my pregnancy. She had plenty of time to turn around, but it was still pretty scary to hear.

MATERNITY CLOTHES SUCK

Now that I was really starting to show, my mom and I decided to go shopping for maternity clothes. I had tried to go once before by myself, but ended up leaving without anything because I felt like people were staring at me. Maternity clothes kind of suck in general, but I figured I would have to wear some eventually.

This time, MTV had planned the trip to a local boutique because they wanted to get some footage of me and my mom shopping together. It wound up being a really emotional experience for me and my mom. It brought up a lot of issues for us and we both ended up bawling our eyes out right in the middle of the store.

As I was looking around, I saw a couple of really cute baby outfits and I was struck by this really strong desire to buy one. Once I knew my baby was a girl, I couldn't help but imagine her in all those cute baby outfits. I told my mom I wished we could buy a couple of outfits, just for the first few days that we would be in the hospital together. I tried to sound casual about it, like it was no big deal, but we both new that the real reason I wanted the clothes was that deep down I was still conflicted about adoption. My mom got really upset and started to cry and then I started crying. My little sister was standing there, witnessing us breaking down, and I felt awful that this decision I had made was affecting my family so drastically. It was all because of my carelessness that we were in this mess in the first place.

She said she was afraid I was going to get too attached to the baby. She had been trying to be strong for me, because she was worried I was going to have a hard time giving up the baby. She didn't want me to suffer, but she felt adoption was the right thing to do because she knew how hard it would be if I tried to raise her on my own as a teenage single mom.

Seeing my mom break down like that made me realize how all of this was affecting her. She had gone through everything I was going through when she got pregnant with me. She was afraid that if I kept my baby, I would end up having to struggle like she did. She didn't want me to buy the outfits because she was trying to protect me from getting too attached. Even though she was more confident about adoption than I was, the process we were going through was hard for my mom, too—after all, this baby would be her granddaughter. I'm sure when she imagined going shopping for baby clothes for her grandchild, she pictured me all grown up and married—not like this. I just felt so sad and guilty for getting myself into this situation.

We cried and hugged each other behind one of the clothes racks. I thought about how hard my mom has had to work to provide for me and my little sister. That made me cry harder because it reminded me that I would never be able to hug my daughter and comfort her as her mother.

Life just sucks sometimes.

DEALING WITH WORK

Pregnant or not, I still had to earn money. I was working at T.J. Maxx, which wasn't so hard at first, but as the pregnancy got father along I began to get intense back pains. It was exhausting being on my feet for six hours at a time. At first I was like, *Okay, wow, I'm lazy!* But then the back pains got worse. I would have to hold my back when I walked and it made me look really awkward. It was such a relief when I was assigned to the fitting room because at least I could kind of lean (even though I wasn't supposed to) and not have to be bending over all the time.

At times work could be just as draining emotionally as it was physically. I remember a lady passing by with her little baby. She was so adorable and she had the cutest cry. It made me so sad, but I tried to shake it off by thinking, *That cry isn't going to be cute at 3:00 A.M.* I thought of all of the reasons why I had chosen adoption. I literally thought over and over, *It's for the best, it's for the best*...because in that moment I desperately wanted to change my mind.

When it became obvious to everyone that I was pregnant, my manager approached me and I confided to her that I was pregnant. She was very supportive and told me she used to teach a sex-ed class. She had met girls as young as fourteen who were pregnant. She admitted she was the one who had been assigning me to the fitting room lately. She was going to put me in another section, but thought to herself, *She looks pregnant*. She stressed the importance of honesty and communication and said that if I was having trouble I should come to her.

On the positive side, there was this young girl I met while I was working out on the floor in the baby department. She was buying baby clothes and we started talking about how cute the clothes were. She said they were for her friend who had just turned nineteen. Somehow we got onto the subject of adoption and I told her what I was going through. She told me that it was such a noble thing for me to do. We just stood there and talked and she reassured me that I was doing the right thing. It honestly helped. Just minutes before I had been on the verge of tears. Even though I said thank you, I don't think she could have known how much our conversation meant to me.

Another positive encounter came at the end of my shift one night. This beautiful woman came into the fitting room. She asked me if I was having a baby. I must have blushed because she apologized right away for asking. I told her that it was fine, it was just that I was only seventeen.

She reassured me that I could get through it and said she admired me. Her words were so inspiring. She smiled and told me to remember that my baby was a blessing from God and assured me that He would take care of it all.

A blessing. I hadn't really thought of it like that before. I had been so focused on the negative that I had lost sight of what a miracle it is to bring a life into the world. Her words reminded me that I must cherish this little life growing inside me because she was a blessing; a bittersweet blessing.

I am so grateful to that woman for being there at that moment. I had been dreading going to work, but I was obviously put there for a reason. She left me with a high five and promised prayers and that was that.

THE LAST FIRST DAY OF SCHOOL

I almost didn't go back for the first day of my senior year. I wasn't planning on going at all, thinking maybe I could graduate before I had to see anyone. I decided to go back, though, and it wasn't that bad. My friend Shelley came over to spend the night the day before the first day of school. She was absolutely great to me during that time. (She was the first friend I told about being pregnant.)

When I got there the following morning, the bell had already rung and it was chaos, which was actually a relief because no one really noticed me. When I left school in the spring, everyone already knew I was pregnant. Now that I was really showing I was nervous how people would react. Since I only needed three credits to graduate, the school decided I could get those in Credit Recovery. They had just built the new high school and they didn't have the

I.S.S (In School Suspension) Credit Recovery teacher yet, so they stuck us all in one room, the I.S.S room, with a substitute teacher. That stunk because I basically thought of I.S.S. Credit Recovery as a program for failing or behind students and I.S.S. as a program for students who had gotten in trouble. So it almost felt like I was getting in trouble for being pregnant. It also meant I wouldn't get to be in class with any of my friends, but this was the only way for me to be done with school before the baby was born.

When I got there they directed me to the wrong class, which was okay because I did get to see some friends I had barely seen all summer. I was relieved that they didn't treat me differently. Everyone just "awwed" at my belly. Some girl I rarely talked to even came up to me and told me I was getting so much bigger.

I was standing by the door of my new class, which was really the wrong one, and I started up a conversation with this kid I had never seen before who was in Credit Recovery, too. He was pretty nice, so it started to seem not that bad after all. Finally, we were directed to our new classroom (the right one). It was a big room with a lot of desks and computers, way more than necessary. The teachers were nice and told us what to expect. I picked my two electives, Humanity/Psychology and a Business Communications class. Then, of course, I had to take my second semester of Senior English. The day flew by. I didn't have to go to my locker or switch classes and I finished the first lesson of my English class.

When it was finally time to leave, I walked out to the cafeteria across the hall and saw a lot of people I hadn't seen in a while. They all had something to say about my new "look." It didn't really bother me because I had had the summer to adjust. Some people I rarely talked to gave me hugs, and one friend even felt my belly and said that she was so sad I wasn't keeping her. It was overwhelming, but I tried not to feel so sad and just the fact that I didn't let it bother me felt like I was making progress and feeling more confident in my decision.

Overall, it wasn't a bad last first day of school. It was fast-paced and emotionally draining. And, of course, I was a little sad I didn't get to be in regular class with all of the new kids and old friends.

After that I just stayed focused. I went in every day and worked at a computer from 9:00 A.M. to noon to complete the credits I needed. I had already taken some community college courses over the summer, so I was definitely on track to finish school before the end of the pregnancy. It wasn't bad—not nearly as bad as I had been afraid it would be. In the end, it was good to graduate early.

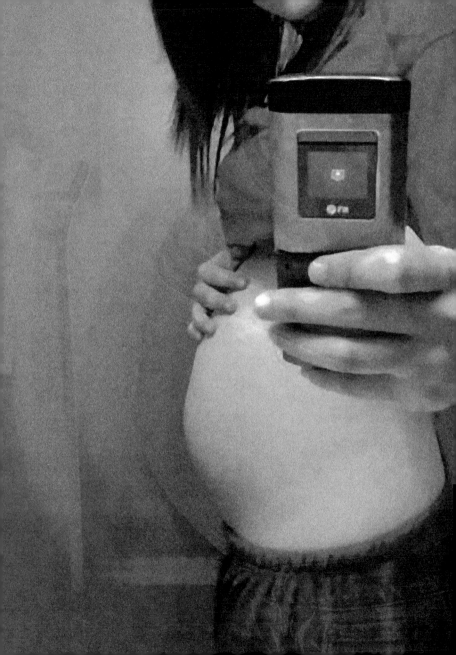

September

JUSTIN'S MOM

Since I had never really met with Justin's mom, Marie, I felt it was time to set the record straight. We met at her house, which was just a few blocks over from mine in McKinney. I showed her the pictures from my ultrasound and explained what I was planning to do. All I have to say is that she is a very nice person and I like her a whole lot. She is honest and open and I admire that about her. She doesn't sugarcoat things. She says what needs to be said. I appreciate that about her. I was so grateful to have her as somebody I could talk to.

She seemed upset by my decision to give the baby up for adoption. I understood that it was hard for her. She loves babies and works at a day care. I think she was really looking forward to being a grandmother, but she understood that it was my decision and that

I had good reasons for making it.

We talked for a while and she showed me Justin's graduation photos. When I saw them, I cried. I wasn't expecting to, but I couldn't help it. He looked so handsome in his cap and gown and I was very proud of him for graduating.

BAD DREAMS

They say you have very intense dreams when you're pregnant. At least in my case, I can say that it was true.

Once I had this really bad dream that totally freaked me out. In it I had already had the baby and had just brought her home from the hospital. We were in front of my house and there were two men dressed in green shirts who really wanted her for some reason. I did everything I could to not let them get near her, but they took her when I wasn't looking. They ran across the street to the neighbors' yard and disappeared.

I had just given birth, so I couldn't move around easily. I tried running after them, but I was too tired and slow. It felt like I was running through water. I screamed for my mom and I grabbed her car keys. I managed to get in her car but couldn't get it to start.

That's when I woke up. Isn't that awful? It ate at me the whole next day and I cried all the way home from class. It was the worst dream I have ever had.

I remember another dream, this one was less disturbing, but it was still very intense. In it I had just had the baby and Justin was there. I didn't want to see her, because I figured it would be too hard to go through with the adoption, so I left and Justin stayed with her. Then I remember going back and looking all over for them. There was some woman with me and she took me to a room of babies, but I didn't know which one was mine. I went around looking at all of them, trying to find the one that looked like Justin. I couldn't find her, so I got frustrated and left. I tried to find Justin to ask him if somebody had taken her and I finally found him at some house party.

I was afraid to go in, but I needed Justin to help me find the baby. So I walked into the party, but when he saw me he ran away. Somehow I caught up with him and started crying. He told me that nobody had taken her and finally agreed to help me look for her. I can't remember exactly how the dream ended, but I remember telling him that I couldn't do it, I couldn't give our baby away, but he was indifferent to whether I did or didn't.

You don't need a degree in psychology to interpret those dreams.

BIRTHMOM

The scariest part about considering adoption was the fear that I wouldn't pick the right couple. The idea of giving my baby to complete strangers was so terrifying. The whole point of choosing adoption over raising her myself was that I wanted her to have the kind of family life I never had growing up. But how could I guarantee that would happen? How could I know for sure the couple I chose really would be the kind of parents I was looking for?

Ashley, the adoption agent from Gladney Center for Adoption, assured me that even though choosing would be difficult, they wanted me to walk away from this experience feeling peaceful about my decision, confident in my adoption plan, and confident in who would be raising my child. I had started looking at profiles of couples on the Gladney website, but I found the whole process too overwhelming. To help me get a better understanding of what was going to happen after my baby was born, the agency arranged for me to meet with a birthmom who had recently gone through the adoption process.

I met with Ashley (yes, another Ashley) at a park in my neighborhood. The MTV crew filmed the meeting and it was one of those moments when being filmed made everything seem strange and surreal. It was awkward at first. Even I was more aware of the camera crew than usual, but after a while we relaxed and forgot they were there. It was helpful to talk with someone who had gone through the adoption process. I felt like she understood where I was coming from and had experienced some of the fears and worries I was having.

Her story of one of her first visitations with her son was very sad. He was four months old and he didn't want her, he wanted his adoptive mother. You could tell how hard that was for her and it broke my heart. Would I be able to stand it when my baby wanted her adoptive mother and not me? How could I not feel angry at the people who had taken my child, even though I was the one who made the decision to give her to them in the first place? The main thing she told me was, "You can't think about yourself. You have to do what's best for your baby." I guess I knew that all along, no matter how hard it was going to be.

The day my baby would be born was going to be one of the worst, yet best, days of my life.

KENNY AND LISA

I was terrified of handing my baby over to strangers. That's why it felt like my prayers were being answered when my mom came to me and told me that her brother, Kenny, and his wife, Lisa, had offered to adopt my baby. They had two older children of their own and had been looking into adopting a third child for a long time. There was a part of me that had been hoping for this, so when my mom told me the news I felt relieved. I hoped it would take away all the confusion I was feeling about adoption.

I thought, *Maybe now we can all be excited without having to worry about getting attached and then having her go to strangers.* If Kenny and Lisa adopted my baby, I would be giving her to people I knew I could trust. I was thankful to them for stepping in.

Kenny and Lisa are amazing parents, the kind I would have liked to have had when I was growing up. They met every single piece of criteria that I had wanted in a family. They have stability (they've been together since they were fifteen years old), they have a self-run, successful business, and both of them work from home. They also have already raised two wonderful kids, my cousins, whom I love very much.

They live in Harlingen, Texas, which is where I lived before we moved to the Dallas area. Growing up I spent a lot of time with Kenny and Lisa and my cousins. They are awesome parents and if they adopted my baby, I would be giving them the third child they had wanted but couldn't have. Also, this way I would know who my baby was growing up around: my own family.

Because we are such a close family, we could be honest with the baby in the future about who I was to her. I knew it was still going to be hard, but at least I knew now that, no matter what, she was not going to go to strangers.

THE PERFECT PLAN

It might seem like having your baby adopted by family would be easier than giving her to strangers, and in a lot of ways it is; I would still be a part of her life, I could see her whenever I wanted, and I knew she would have a great life. But in many ways it would make it even more difficult for me. While everyone else's roles would stay the same (my mom would still be like a grandma and my sister would still be her auntie) mine would be different in a way that I wasn't sure I could handle.

Even though I tried to ignore the creeping doubts, questions and fears swirled around in my mind, especially as my due date got closer. It was so hard to wrap my mind around giving her up—to anyone. A huge part of me felt like I could keep her, with help from my mom, but I also had dreams and I still wanted to make a future for myself, especially if I kept her.

Even though I knew it wouldn't be fair to my aunt and uncle, I couldn't help imagining how great it would be if I just had a few years to get school out of the way. I could get a decent job to support us both. But then, what if I did take time to build a future and then came back for her? Maybe she wouldn't want to leave. I would be ripping her from everything she knew. Even if she did want to go with me, it would cause conflict and confusion for everyone.

On the other hand, even if my mom helped me raise her, there would still be complications. That's what happened when I was little. My mom had to rely on her parents for help raising me and it caused a lot of conflict between all of us. I didn't want that for me and my daughter. I didn't want to put our relationship in jeopardy, or my mom's and mine.

Even if things went in the best possible way, there would still be the absence of a father. It is important to me that my baby have two parents. For years I cried every Father's Day because it hurt that much not to have ever really known my biological father. I didn't want my baby to have to go through that.

If I raised her myself. I wouldn't be around enough because I would be finishing school and working to support us. She would have to be with a nanny or put into day care. That's not what I wanted for her. I believe a child should be raised by its parents.

I didn't have the money or education my aunt and uncle have. I couldn't provide the kind of stable home they already had in place. It would have been great to say love is enough, but it hurt knowing I couldn't give my baby anything and everything she might need.

With Kenny and Lisa in the picture, now more than ever my decision boiled down to choosing between what would be less painful for me versus what would be best for my baby. If I decided to keep her, it would be out of selfishness: to avoid the sadness of giving her up. If I kept her, she would end up suffering along with me, but if Kenny and Lisa adopted her it would just be me that had to suffer. She would be happy in a stable home with two loving parents. In the end, I decided I would rather suffer alone.

NEW YORK?

Now that I had a plan in place for my baby's future, I started thinking about what I would do after all this was behind me. One of the positive things about this process was that it forced me to think about my future for the first time. I definitely wanted to see more of the world than McKinney, Texas.

Getting pregnant was a wake up call. I realized I had no plan for my future. I had been coasting through life. Now, it was time to think about where I was headed and how I was going to get there.

I had wanted to go to New York City forever. It just seemed exciting and different, like if I went there I'd be doing something positive with my life. The scary part was just doing it.

Moving there all by myself and being on my own in such a big city was scary to contemplate. It's such an intimidating place to an eighteen-year-old with no life experience. As much as I wanted to go, I was scared. Scared out of my Miinnddd!!

The director of my episode of *16 and Pregnant* went to grad school at The New School in Manhattan and she highly recommended it. I started thinking that maybe it was a good fit for me. Honestly, I didn't have time to thoroughly research schools so when it came down to crunch time (just a couple of weeks) to apply, it was the only one I knew.

The one thing I was one hundred percent confident about was that I wanted to major in film production. I had always been into photojournalism and I love taking photographs and writing. My experience with MTV got me interested in film production. They have a good film program at The New School, so I hoped it would end up being the perfect school for me.

SAT time was coming around. The score on this test is a factor that can determine what colleges you get into. I took practice tests and did well, but, although my score did end up being high enough to get me into The New School, in the end I didn't do as well as I had hoped. When I took the test I was about to go into labor. I could barely fit in the desk and everybody was staring at me. I didn't even have the right calculator.

The whole planning-for-the-future thing was definitely stressful. A big part of me didn't want to deal with or think about life after the pregnancy, but the weeks were flying by and there was so much pressure to make so many different decisions.

I wasn't sure at this point exactly where I was going to end up, but I just felt like I needed to get out of Texas. I'd stopped hanging out with most of my friends, Justin and I were over, and I really felt like there was nothing for me at home. I needed a change and it needed to be big.

Looking back, I have to admit that a large part of wanting to make such a drastic move had to do with me trying to run away after the baby was born. But at the time I desperately felt that I needed to have a plan for what was going to happen after the pregnancy.

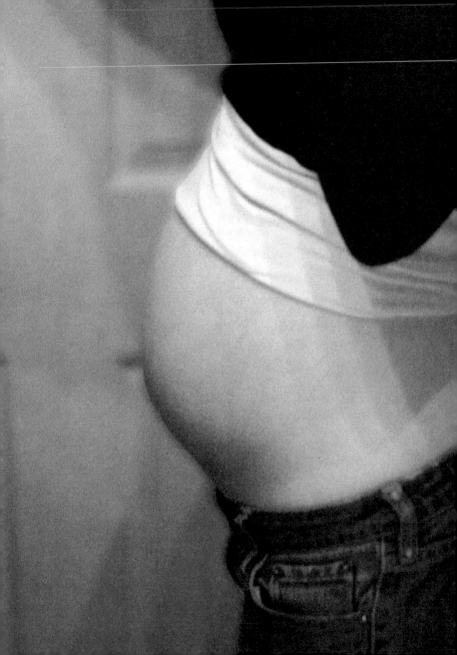

October

BACK PAIN

Meanwhile, despite all the drama I had going on in my life, with all the decisions I had to make that would forever change the course of my future, there was still the simple everyday reality that I was pregnant. A life was steadily growing inside me, changing my body as it was getting ready to be born.

At twenty-eight weeks I had another doctor's appointment. I found out I was anemic, which meant that I didn't have enough red blood cells to circulate oxygen through my body. That accounted for some of the exhaustion I was feeling. My doctor said it was normal for this point in my pregnancy and told me start taking iron pills.

I also had to go through Glucose testing. This is when they test you for gestational diabetes, which is a kind of diabetes you can get when you're pregnant. They make you drink this disgusting syrup, like a thick coke without carbonation, and wait an hour and then test your blood. If it's high, you have to come back, do it again, and get tested every hour for three hours. Thankfully, my results came back excellent and I didn't have to do that. The baby was still breech, but my doctor said that less than seven percent of babies don't turn around and he assured me I should be okay.

The only really difficult thing was that my back pain was becoming unbearable. During the ultrasound it was hurting so badly I felt like I was going to throw up. The nurse and my mom helped me to sit up for a few minutes, and that helped a little. It was weird because I had never had much morning sickness or had felt that close to throwing up before. The doctor explained that when you lay on your back, the baby is big enough to put pressure on an artery and can block oxygen to the heart, which can cause nausea.

I was starting to feel ready for my body to return back to normal and for this to be over. The weight gain was definitely a beating. I was still in all my old pants/clothes, but I guess it was the number that freaked me out. By the end of my pregnancy I weighed around 170 lbs!

I was also pretty stressed about going through labor. The whole process was terrifying to think about. How much would it hurt? What if something went wrong? What if there wasn't enough time for the epidural? Not to mention the fact that once she was born, I would really have to deal with the reality of giving her away.

I did love the feeling of the baby moving and kicking. So in a way, I didn't want it to be over that soon.

UNBORN BABIES

Something I thought about all the time was, *Can unborn babies sense emotions from the inside?* Every time I argued with someone, cried, or felt sad, I ended up crying even more out of stress and guilt. I felt so guilty because I was afraid the baby could sense what I was feeling and would absorb all those emotions.

Pregnant women are supposed to do yoga and listen to classical music so that their babies will develop in a calm, stress-free environment. They're not supposed to be crying, confused and stressed out all the time. That can't be good for a developing baby. Sometimes I would even get cramps when I was feeling especially overwhelmed or sad. Maybe it was just the stress itself. There's no telling. But it really made me feel completely awful and guilty.

TIME TO GROW UP

My decision to share my experience of being a pregnant teen so publicly (through my blog and by appearing on *16 and Pregnant*), had both a positive and negative impact on my life. It made me realize how many different kinds of people are out there. People that are willing to help you and offer a caring word or two, but also people that are ready to criticize and tear you down.

My blog really brought that second group of folks out. People can be so much meaner in cyberspace than they would ever be in real life, to your face. When you have an open blog, people who don't even know you feel that they have the right to condemn you for the choices you make. Here's the kind of criticism I got on my blog after I posted about deciding on adoption:

I'd just like to say, I am a teen mother, I was 16 and pregnant and I think it is wonderful that you're giving your baby up for adoption, rather than aborting the life you've created, but it seems you're doing it for selfish reasons! Yes you may have had dreams, and blah blah, but you set those aside when you opened your legs... You don't sound ready, so bless your baby!

It starts out like it's going to be a positive comment, but then *wham!* she gets a punch in. That's how it feels, when someone posts a negative comment—like they've punched you in the stomach. When I first started my blog, I never thought about how it was going to be a dialogue between me and other people. I learned fast. The comments can be very cruel and you have to have a thick skin. Fortunately, there were more positive comments than negative ones and most people were very supportive.

Having such a public dialogue about my choice opened my eyes to the realities of my life. Getting a lot of criticism from strangers about how I was handling things forced me to really look at myself and to be honest about what I was seeing.

And what I saw was this: I still lived at home with my mom and I had no means to support myself, much less a baby. All I really had to do was the dishes, and honestly sometimes I couldn't even do that. I didn't know how I was ever going to make it on my own. I couldn't even take care of myself. I couldn't cook, unless you count macaroni and cheese or cereal as a meal. I couldn't even properly clean sometimes. I lacked initiative and determination.

I'm not tearing myself apart. I'm just being honest about where I was at that point in my life. This pregnancy pushed me to grow up. I had to make decisions I would never have had to make otherwise. Some of which were decisions that nobody should ever have to make.

I think if I hadn't grown up in that sense, I probably would have kept my baby. It takes a lot of maturity to make a decision like I did. The grown-up in me saw a happy future for my baby if she had a stable home life. The baby in me wanted to make selfish choices to avoid feeling sad and lonely.

I was also motivated to do things I would never have otherwise had the courage to do. Like go forward with applying to colleges in New York. When I focused on that, it made me feel good.

November

HEARTBURN

At thirty-one weeks I learned the true meaning of the word heartburn. It was horrible. I'd never experienced anything like that before. At the beginning of the pregnancy, I would get minor cases that didn't last very long, but this was so much worse. It hurt in my upper back, too. It felt awful and seemed to last forever.

I remember my mom saying, "If you can't handle this..." and leaving it at that. Obviously, she meant that if I couldn't handle the heartburn, how was I going to deal with the labor and delivery? I was definitely terrified about the labor, but then I think that's normal for most women.

FROM THE HOSPITAL TO THE PRINCETON REVIEW

On Monday, November 22nd, 2009 (which strangely enough was Justin's birthday) at around 8:00 A.M., I started having contractions. They were inconsistent and I was only thirty-six weeks, so I ignored them. They started getting more and more consistent around 10:00 P.M., from six minutes, to four, to three, to two, to one. I thought my water had even broken, so I called my doctor and ended up going to the ER at 1:00 A.M.

They kept me overnight with "irritability," which are minor contractions. The baby's heart rate was also up and I was dehydrated, so they put me on an IV with a water-type solution. After that, the contractions weren't stopping so they tried putting me on some other type of IV fluid. In the end, I wound up getting three shots of something, I don't even remember the name. It stung really bad going in. It was miserable. I really hate hospitals. I had to spend the whole next day there, still on an IV. I did get an ultrasound, though, and that was really cool because it was 3D. It was crazy to see the baby's facial features so clearly. They ended up sending me home with some capsule/pill things to bring down my blood pressure. I had to take them every six hours until the bottle ran out.

I hated those things. I felt like they made my heart race. I would get shaky and had to check my pulse regularly. I would even wake up in the middle of the night to check it. Once, I got so shaky I had to miss class. They switched me between two medicines, but they were both awful.

Later that day, after I was released from the hospital, I got to meet with Rob Franek of the Princeton Review. He is an awesome guy. He had so much information and helped me with my questions about college. You could tell that he loves what he does.

He encouraged me to visit the schools I was interested in because I would have an instant reaction to the right one and would know that it was the place for me.

JUSTIN EMERGES

After five months of no contact, I finally met with Justin face to face. He had told one of his friends that he wanted to see me and apologize. I was worried it was going to be awkward and, honestly, it was.

When he saw me, the first thing he did was give me a hug and ask if the baby moved a lot and if she was moving right then. He said he was excited to have a baby on the way. He was just sad that we weren't in the right place in our lives. It wasn't that he didn't want anything to do with her. He apologized for not being there for me. I could tell he meant it.

Everything he told me about how he'd been living made me feel sorry for him. His mom had kicked him out and he'd been bouncing around from place to place. The night before he had slept in his friend's car. When he told me that, it broke my heart. He told me that he knew it had been hard for me, but I was thinking, I would rather be pregnant for nine months with the security of a house, my mom, a warm bed, and shower, than go through what he was experiencing.

What really surprised me was that he kept referring to the baby as *his kid*, *his daughter* and even *our daughter*. I never expected him to feel that connected to her. He told me that if things were different, if he had the money, if his life were more together, he would have definitely wanted to be a part of her life. I could tell he was sincere. He knew how hard it was to grow up not knowing your father.

We talked about how we had considered abortion in the beginning and, even though it had seemed to him like the right choice at the time, we were both glad we hadn't gone that route. The whole time he was just very apologetic. I have never had anyone apologize to me that many times or seem as sincere as he was. He was staring at me the whole time, which made it awkward, but also very sad. I could see in his eyes how sad he was and how something had clicked inside him.

He also surprised me by saying he'd like to see the baby before the adoption was final. I think that he was very confused. We both were. I saw a whole different side of him that day and I really hoped he would fix his life up. When I asked him how he felt about my decision to pursue adoption I thought maybe he wouldn't know how to respond. I was surprised to learn that he felt the same way I did. He wanted his child to have the kind stability from two loving parents that he never had growing up. Seeing him again helped me feel more confident in my decision to go through with adoption because this baby deserved a better life than what Justin and I were dealt.

That night he signed the adoption papers. I had wanted to go, but my mom wouldn't let me. The MTV crew was there to film it, but it didn't make the cut for the episode.

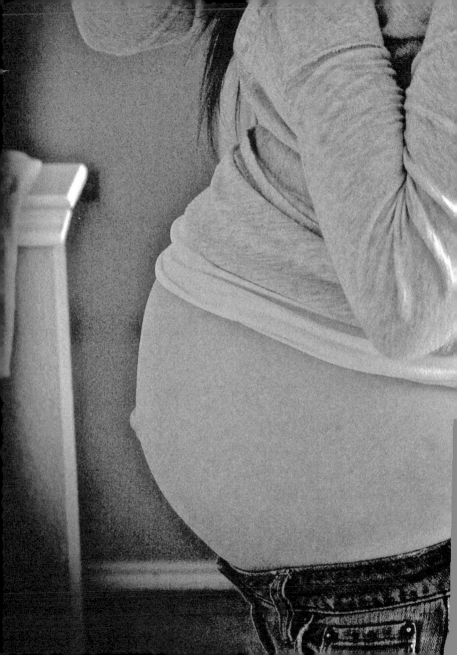

December

INDUCTION

My original due date was December 22nd, 2009 and one of the things I was worried about was forever associating Christmas, which is a big holiday in my family, with giving up my baby. I talked about it with my doctor and he and I decided that I could be induced early. We settled on Wednesday, December 16th and arranged that I would go to the hospital the evening before, so my mom could come with me after she finished work.

I arrived at the hospital at 10:00 P.M. on the 15th of December. I got my IV needle in and filled out some basic paperwork. Since I wasn't dilated at all, they inserted a weird pill in me that would help dilate me and start off the labor process. My mom stayed the night with me and in the morning they started me on Pitocin, the drug they use to bring on contractions.

As soon as the pain started, they gave me an epidural, which came with a pump that allowed me to control how much of the medication I got. I kept it at a moderate level, so that I could feel the contractions at least a little bit. Then they gave me Nubain, a pain medication, and boy did it make me loopy! My Mimi came to visit and told me later that I was saying all sorts of bizarre things. Even the film crew was making fun of me. I needed it though. It was like I could feel the baby's wrist grinding into my abdomen.

One of the hardest moments during that part of my labor was when the nurse put a red hospital ID bracelet on my arm. I wasn't sure what it was for because I already had an ID bracelet on. When I asked the nurse, she explained that my baby would have a matching one put on her wrist after she was born. She said, "This is for identification. It means *this baby* belongs to *this mommy*."

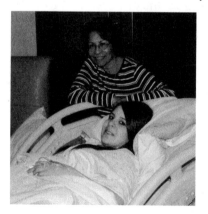

Obviously, she didn't know about my situation. Despite my loopy Nubain state, hearing that still made me sad because I was thinking, *But this baby won't belong to this mommy. She'll belong to someone else.* I looked over at my mom and I could tell that she knew what I was thinking. Now I was even more scared and anxious than ever about giving birth.

Meanwhile, the hospital was clued in for the first time that this was an adoption situation when a woman came to talk to us about birth certificates. We informed her that, since this was a family adoption, I didn't have an adoption agent, so they sent a social worker to talk to me. The social worker was nice, but I found the whole thing kind of surreal. She asked me why I had chosen adoption and I gave her the same answers I had been giving over and over to everyone—*I'm too young, I can't offer her stability, I want her to have two parents.* Only now, saying those things while I was in labor and about to see my baby for the first time felt false. I wanted her. She was *my* baby. I was the one struggling to deliver her. I was the one who couldn't wait to see what she looked like.

She asked me if I planned to spend time with the baby before the adoption was finalized. I said, "Yes, as much time as possible." I could tell from the look on her face that this was a red flag that I wasn't confident about my decision. For me, it was just beginning to hit home that this process was going to be so much more agonizing than I could possibly have imagined. I had known it was going to be hard. I had been telling everyone that I understood it was going to be hard. But I didn't realize until that moment just how impossibly hard it was going to be.

As the day wore on, my labor was progressing even if I couldn't really feel it. Meanwhile, I had a lot of visitors to cheer me up and, of course, the MTV crew to keep me company. In fact, when I wasn't sad, I was kind of bored all day, sitting in my hospital bed with the Pitocin IV stuck in my arm. Honestly, I was napping right before she was born.

The nurse woke me up and said it was time to check how dilated I was. Then, all of a sudden, she was saying it was time to push. Since the baby wasn't getting enough oxygen, they put an O2 mask on me, but I kept moving it aside without realizing it. I pushed for about forty-five minutes and the pain wasn't terrible, except when her elbow, or maybe it was her wrist, was pressing into me. In the end, I was in active labor for about an hour and a half.

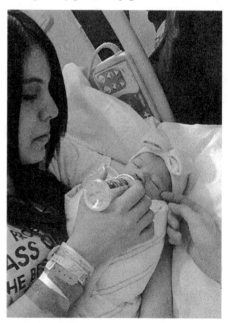

Callie Danielle Salazar was finally born at 6:48 P.M. that evening. Kenny and Lisa chose her name. I didn't feel like it was my place to make that decision. Coincidentally, Lisa and I share the middle name Danielle, so Lisa decided it would be a special way to honor the connection between the three of us if Callie also had Danielle as her middle name. I loved that idea and was very happy that she and I would share two of her names—Danielle and Salazar.

Let me tell you, labor isn't fun. There's a lot of blood and other gross fluids. I even threw up a couple of times. Even after the baby is born, it's hard. You're exhausted and in excruciating pain, especially if you have to have an episiotomy—which is when they have to cut you to help the baby come out. Even though I didn't have a whole lot of pain during delivery, I lost a lot of blood and that made it even more exhausting.

Afterwards, I was limp in one leg and the nurses had to help me get out of bed and into a wheelchair to get to my post-labor room. After the nurses took Callie away to run some tests, I tried to eat a little food that the MTV crew had brought me but passed out mid-sandwich. I remember Justin's mom came by at one point, but I fell asleep while she was talking. I have never been so tired in my life.

SO PERFECT

It was worth it, though! The moment Callie was born, they put her right in my arms. She was so pretty, no scratches or bruises from the delivery. Her skin was so soft. No blemishes. Nothing. She was so perfect. She slept peacefully, never cried, and was the cutest thing I'd ever seen.

Babies are so innocent. Holding Callie in my arms,

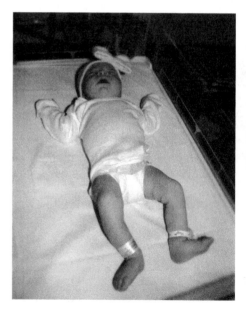

watching her coo and wriggle, while I lay there crying, I was relieved that she was untouched by the turmoil of emotions I was experiencing. I was definitely in a state of shock. I kept looking at her and thinking, *Is this really happening?* I felt so lost, small, and helpless.   I never knew that loving somebody so much was possible. And she loved me, too. On some instinctive level she knew I was her mother. I could tell when she looked at me with her pretty dark blue eyes—Justin's eyes.

It's true what they say: There is no other love like a mother's love for her baby.

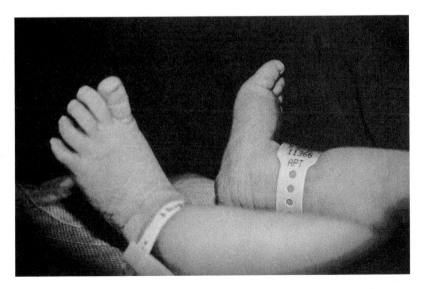

THE FIRST 48 HOURS

According to Texas state law, you can't sign adoption papers until forty-eight hours after a child is born. It's not literally forty-eight hours, though. For example, Callie was born at 6:48 P.M. on December 16th, but I didn't have to wait until 6:48 P.M. on December 18th to sign the papers. But, in my mind, the state of Texas was giving me forty-eight hours to shut everything else out and enjoy my baby and I planned to take every single second I had with her.

I had been warned (by my mother, by people on my blog, by other birth mothers) that once I saw my baby it would become much more difficult to follow through with my adoption plan. Now I was learning just how true those words were. I don't know how many times I went back and forth with my decision once Callie was born. While I was in the hospital, I didn't stick to one emotion for more than an hour. I felt angry, sad, upset, happy, confused and confident about things all at the same time. I was so exhausted from the loss of blood during delivery and the lack of sleep afterward that half the time I didn't know what I was saying or doing.

The one thing I was one hundred percent sure about was that I wanted to soak up every moment I had with Callie. I wanted to try to do everything for her myself. I even got annoyed with the nurses when they insisted on taking her away the first night because of the high risk of choking for newborns in the first twenty-four hours. I got a couple of hours of sleep that night, but took Callie back as soon as I could so as not to waste a single precious moment.

That next day, I couldn't do as much as I had hoped. I was so exhausted and overwhelmed. I got up, took a shower, and did my hair and makeup (I was being filmed every moment of the day, after all). I fed and changed Callie, but needed a lot of help from my mom. I was frustrated that I didn't know more about how to take care of her. I wanted so badly to prove (at least to myself) that I could be a good mom. So that night, I stayed up as long as I could, feeding Callie every three hours. Finally, at around 4:00 A.M. the nurse gave me some pain medicine that made me drowsy. Since the baby's nurse had to do another check-up on her, I let them take her so I could get some rest. I slept for a couple of hours and got up at 6:00 A.M., exhausted but determined to continue feeding and taking care of Callie. I was proud of myself. I was actually learning and was at the point where I could feed and change her without help. I felt like if someone else did it, I was being useless. I enjoyed the sense of accomplishment that taking care of her on my own gave me.

I was so tired, though, that I nodded off with her in my arms at one point. It was scary—like I couldn't let her go for anything. I didn't want that last day to end. I wanted to keep Callie, but a voice in my head was telling me that it wouldn't be the best thing for her. So I stayed in the hospital as long as I could, desperately trying to put off dealing with the inevitable.

It was particularly hard when Kenny and Lisa came to visit. I knew they were trying to balance wanting to see Callie with trying to be sensitive to my feelings, but I couldn't help feeling possessive. I asked my mom to tell them to leave. I felt awful, but it was just too painful for me to have them there. This was supposed to be *my* time with Callie.

They both left crying and my mom had to remind me that Kenny and Lisa were not the enemy. It was hard for her because she was caught between trying to do what was best for me and worrying about her brother (not to mention dealing with the rest of our family putting in their two cents). By now the stress of what we were going through, along with having a camera in her face, was beginning to weigh on my mom.

The stress was taking a toll on me, too. I changed my mind a million times while I was in the hospital. I talked with the doctor, the nurses, my family, even the crew, about my increasing sense of doubt about the adoption. Then I finally had to talk to my mom and explain what was going on in my head. We talked about my childhood and how the lack of stability I had has always been a big issue for me. She reminded me that, if I chose to raise Callie myself, her experience would be just like mine. My childhood wasn't horrible, but I wanted a better life for Callie. Another thing I worried about was how it would impact my relationship with my mom. Just like my grandparents helped raise me, my mom would have to help me with Callie and that was bound to cause tension between us in terms of who was the real parent.

After that, there were even more difficult moments in the hospital. The worst of which was filling out Callie's birth certificate. I remember the hospital social worker explaining that, since this was an adoption, the adoptive parents would apply for a new birth certificate once the papers were signed. The new certificate would have their names on it as the mother and father. My name wouldn't be on it at all. That was painful to hear. No one had explained to me that Callie would have two birth certificates and that my name would only be on the original one. I had just brought this beautiful baby into the world and now my name, my part in giving her life, was going to be erased.

I agonized for the rest of my time in the hospital. It had all seemed so much simpler before she was born. Although I had been conflicted, I had felt more confident that Kenny and Lisa adopting

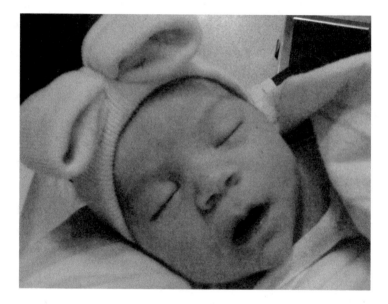

her was the right thing to do. Then Callie came into the world and I fell in love. Suddenly, the decision I had made became more than hard—it was unbearable. That night my Mimi and Papa came to visit and told me that they had faith in me. But they stressed that I needed to make a wise decision. I felt like everyone was giving me conflicting advice: we know you can do it, but do what's best for the baby.

Finally, the afternoon I was supposed to leave the hospital, my mom and I had a final talk. There was no way to be objective about the baby in my arms. I already loved Callie more than I have ever loved anyone. In my heart I knew I wanted to keep her, but all the reasons my mom brought up for going through with the adoption weighed on me. My mom was sympathetic but now, looking back, I feel like she pressured me. I just wish she had said, "Ashley, you can do this and you will do great if you decide to." That was all I would have needed to hear. But she never said that.

Instead, she said that Kenny and Lisa would be okay with whatever I decided and that she would support whatever decision I made. But…she wanted me to make the decision for Callie, not for me. I knew then what she really thought I should do: let Kenny and Lisa adopt Callie.

So that's what I did.

That's when things got really stressful, especially with the MTV crew filming everything. I felt so much anger boiling to the surface as I was packing Callie up and getting her dressed to leave the hospital. I was bawling my eyes out and tried to kick the film crew out. Out of respect they did leave for a few minutes, but they had a job to do and documenting my experience, particularly these painful moments, was the point of why they were there. After they came back, I noticed one of the crew crying, mascara running down her cheeks as she filmed from behind the curtain separating the sitting room from my part of the room. I had grown close to the crew and my producer (who had to stand with a tiny monitor and watch everything being filmed from both camera angles) so they were swept up in how sad and painful this moment was for me.

When the hospital released me, I was taken out in a wheelchair (it was hospital policy) even though I could walk. I remember trying to hide my face from the cameras with my sister's *Nightmare Before Christmas* blanket. We put Callie into her car seat and drove straight to my aunt Jen's house to sign the papers. I sat in the backseat with Callie, crying the whole way there. I was sleep-deprived and still out of it from all the medications. When we got there, my mom took Callie inside and told me to take my time. I stayed in the car sobbing for a while. I knew I had to pull it together, so eventually I got out and went into the house.

The notary had arrived and gave me the papers to sign. There had been many painful moments in the past few months and days, but signing the adoption papers was hands down the saddest moment of my life. My contacts felt glued to my eyes and when I started crying it made my vision worse. I'm glad it did though, because the few words I did see on the paper were "…forever terminate my rights to the child."

There were so many pages and the wording was so dense. It was more than I could handle. So I didn't read it, I just flipped the pages and signed where I was supposed to sign. It was the most heart-wrenching thing I ever had to do, but I just had to keep thinking about Callie and not myself. It must have been a difficult moment for everyone, because when I looked up I saw that almost everyone was crying. My mom was crying, my aunt was crying—even the film crew was crying.

Then we put Callie into Lisa's arms and my mom drove me home. That night, and for the next few nights, I cried and slept and cried 'til my eyes were so swollen I could barely open them. My mom had to come in and lay down with me because I was having horrible nightmares and she could hear me crying in my sleep.

SECOND THOUGHTS

After signing the papers, I experienced a flood of emotions: anger, sadness, relief, devastation, terror, pride, disappointment in myself. I was miserable. I felt like I had made the wrong decision, that I had made a huge mistake.

I felt like I was stopped in the middle of a huge crowd of people, with everyone moving all around me. I was paralyzed in the middle of it all with everything moving at super top speed, like film fast forwarding. I couldn't do anything but watch and wonder why I couldn't move forward, too. I saw people laughing and going about their days like nothing was wrong at all. I wanted to join them so badly, but I couldn't move on. It felt never-ending. I was confused. The sadness would sneak up on me when I least expected it, making time pass as fast or as slow as it wanted. It was out of my control.

Once I came home from the hospital, I couldn't stop crying. The few moments I did feel happy I also felt guilty because I felt like I didn't have the right to feel anything good.

I wanted to sleep all day and night and never get up. When I was asleep I had horrible dreams and when I was awake I was filled with regret. It was so hard, to feel so much heartache and yet be thinking that the thing that made you feel this way was the right thing to do. I felt like I could have been a good mom to Callie, but if I went back on my decision I would be going back on everything I said I wanted for her. As confused as I was before Callie was born, this was even more complicated.

I thought maybe it was the maternal feelings I was having that were making it so hard for me to let go. My love for Callie was so powerful and intense. In the hospital, it felt like a warm blanket I could wrap us both up in. But now that she was gone, I felt cold, alone, and exposed. The only thing I had to cling to was the idea that I had given Callie up so that she could have a better life than I could give her. But it was getting harder and harder to keep that in sight when the pain of not having her with me was so intense.

It was like a death, except when someone dies you can't see that person again. I could see Callie again, but I still felt the kind of pain you feel when someone is gone forever. I loved her. I wanted her. I would have done anything in the world for her. I didn't know what was right and wrong anymore. I just knew that I missed her and I wanted her with me.

I wanted to hear her cry because she needed to be changed or because she was hungry. I wanted to skip years ahead and be the one she came home to when she was sad or needed comfort, or when she had the best news in the world so I could congratulate her. I wanted her to be sixteen so I could throw the best party for her. I wanted her to be seventeen so I could see her off to her first prom. I wanted her to get in trouble so I could teach her right from wrong. I wanted to protect her. I wanted to be called mom, not Ashley.

I didn't know what the future held for me. All I knew was that I had to keep going and start my future and do it for Callie. Otherwise my decision to go through with the adoption would have been pointless. I told myself I just had to take it day by day. I felt that she was well taken care of and in the best hands possible, but there really wasn't any way to not worry or feel sad. Nothing was clear in those days. Nothing.

CLEARING THINGS UP

As I was struggling with all of this, a lot of people were leaving negative comments on my blog. Many insisted that adoption is wrong for everybody, that only those in extreme circumstances should choose adoption. They said that birth mothers who give up their children are selfish and adopted children never get over feeling abandoned. I tried over and over again to explain that I was doing this for Callie, not me, but the negative posts just kept rolling in.

Some of the comments were thoughtful and heartfelt, but most of them were just malicious. Given my state of mind, it was tough to read through them. I already had so many doubts and reading and responding to these posts was a lot like the argument I was constantly having with myself. It's hard enough to go through the experience of giving up a child, but the negative comments left me feeling like I was, at best, a failure and, at worst, selfish.

The weight of this dialogue was clear to my mom, who felt compelled to step up to try to stave off the attacks. She wrote the following post in my defense. Though I didn't necessarily agree with all the opinions she expressed, I was very grateful to her.

A letter from mom:

This is the first time I'm writing a comment and I wasn't planning to, but I see what pain my daughter is in. She is trying to cope with the hardest decision ever...Mothers want what is best for their children. That's all I have ever wanted for my daughter and I know that is all my daughter wanted for hers. You don't know anything about Ashley or her family. So I feel like it is my responsibility to tell you...

Ok, so Ashley got pregnant on April 1ˢᵗ, 2009. We sat down and discussed her options. I want you to know that she immediately took abortion off her list. We discussed adoption vs. parenting. We had many discussions. We made lists of pros and cons. I am a single mom. There is only so much that I could provide financially and with a 12-year-old and a very demanding full-time job I could not commit to babysitting. Ashley wasn't thinking about herself at all. She was thinking about Callie first and foremost and then about everyone else she was affecting.

I have always worked demanding jobs that have kept me away from home a lot. Ashley's father has never consistently been a part of her life. This has affected her tremendously. Callie was going to have an absent father as well. This was a very big concern for Ashley. She cries every Fathers Day. She cries when she sees daddies and daughters spending time together. She desperately wanted Callie to have the stability she felt she lacked growing up. I did remarry when Ashley was four, and my ex-husband raised her from four years old 'til we divorced when she was 16. He promised that he would always be her father, but then he moved 550 miles away. He only took responsibility for our 12 yr old (his biological daughter). Once again she felt abandoned...

Along with the resentment she carries around for her absent father, she also resents me for never being there. She saw a pattern that she was going to repeat. She loves Callie so much that she did not want her to experience that either. I know it means nothing to you but it does to Ashley. She is young. She needs to go to college and she will also have to work, leaving very little time for Callie. There is also a very negative energy in our home. Ashley and I have a very troubled relationship that we are trying to repair...Ashley did not want Callie to be around the arguing. Again we are working on repairing it but you can't fix years of anger and resentment over-night.

Other reasons: My twelve-year-old, financial issues, no child support, college education, insurance...I'm overextended and Ashley knows it. Maybe I have failed her once again but she was just trying to make the best decision for Callie.

She desperately loves her. She is not exploiting her. I take full responsibility for the blog. When Ashley got pregnant I encouraged her to blog about her feelings so she wouldn't keep them bottled-up. The blog came way before MTV. Ashley really wanted to reach out to teens after becoming pregnant. She was feeling the pain of kids at school ridiculing her and snickering...She realized that pregnancy is not glamorous and movies and shows like Juno *and* The Secret Life of the American Teenager *were not portraying an accurate picture of teen pregnancy. She just wanted to get the word out there. She wanted to send out a warning to teen girls. Then another teen girl came to her and told her about* 16 and Pregnant. *After researching what the show was about, I gave Ashley my consent to apply. This show is a documentary. They too are trying to paint a real picture of teen pregnancy. They have not influenced Ashley in any way with her decision. They have never given us a script or told us what to say. It is true life. Ashley's struggles are real.*

Let's change gears now. Let's talk about the birth and the adop-

tion. *I will tell you that the three days we spent in the hospital and the week after were the most heart-wrenching days that I have EVER experienced in my life. Ashley was confident with her adoption plan prior to the birth. My brother and sister-in-law were a Godsend. When they stepped in, we decided to go with a private attorney vs. the agency that was giving Ashley incredible support and counseling. When we left the agency, the counseling stopped. Ashley was unprepared for the birth and how that whole experience was going to affect her. She had decided that since she would always be in Callie's life, it would be ok to spend 48 hours in the hospital with Callie prior to signing. I was so worried because I know what it is like to see your baby for the first time and how amazing birth is. I knew that it would make going through with her adoption plan very difficult.*

Well, I was right. We checked in to the hospital on a Tuesday night and did not get good sleep again till we were discharged on Friday. Ashley had some complications during delivery, which wore her out even more. From the moment Ashley laid eyes on Callie, her confidence and decision went out the window. She cried for the next few days. She loved Callie as much as she could. She prolonged discharge. Because the agency was out of the picture, I became the middle-man. When you have a close family like we do, you worry about everyone's feelings. My brother and his wife came up and were staying with my sister. My parents were there as well. Everyone was calling me to see how Ashley was, and they all wanted to know if she was sticking to her decision. I will tell you the best people were my brother and his wife. They did not push; they just wanted what was best for Ashley...I was the one that pressed. I lost sight of Ashley's feelings. I was concerned with the 48 hours and that it would be time to sign away her rights. I was thinking about my brother. I told Ashley that her time was up and she needed to make a decision. I told her that my brother needed to know if they were going home with Callie or not. I forgot to listen. She was desperate and delirious. Her eyes were so swollen from all the crying she couldn't even see straight. She kept saying "Mom I don't know, I need more time with Callie." I didn't hear her. Well, she felt pressured, so she gave Callie to them.

But what came next was the most devastating thing that I have ever had to experience. To see my daughter lying there in pain and agony, not wanting to live anymore, just killed me. I didn't know what to do. I reached out to the social worker from the original adoption agency. She said that the agency would have never allowed her to sign if they would have been there. All of the things Ashley was saying were red flags. They would have had an attorney present at signing, along with other things that did not happen as they should have...

Ashley decided that she would rather take all the pain for Callie than have her daughter have the same experience she did growing up. She is having a very hard time with this decision but she has peace knowing that Callie is happy where she is. She has so much love. My parents are five minutes away. All of my aunts, uncles and cousins are where she is. We will all play our same roles. My 12 yr old is still Auntie, I am still Grandma and Callie will know that Ashley is her mama. Callie will be blessed because she will also have my brother and his wife to call mom and most importantly Daddy!

I am very proud of Ashley! She has made a very selfless and mature decision. Yes I know that she has shared something very private with the world, but we hope that it will bring some awareness to young teens out there that are considering pregnancy! There is NOTHING glamorous about teen pregnancy!

I was so happy that my mom posted that letter. The more I tried to defend myself, the less convinced I was that I knew what I was doing. Having a baby and contemplating what it would take to raise her on my own made me realize how hard my mom has had it. I realize now how much she has sacrificed and I can appreciate all that she has done for my sister and me.

It was bad enough that people were attacking me on my blog, but I felt awful when they started attacking my aunt and uncle.

They weren't the ones to blame for why I was so conflicted. All along they had done their best not to put pressure on me. They were very respectful about giving me time with Callie and only came to the hospital after she was born when I said it was okay. My main conflict was not feeling at peace with my decision after I gave Callie to them. I didn't speak up with what I wanted, and I should have.

No matter how difficult all of this was for me, I knew without a doubt that my aunt and uncle would love my daughter just as much as I did. They would never stand in the way of me having a relationship with her and there would never be a need for scheduled visitations. If I wanted to see her tomorrow, I could. If I went back home and felt sad and wanted to see her again soon, I could. There was no "every six months" or "twice a year" type deal. She's family. They are family.

I chose adoption because I felt it was the right thing at the time. When Callie was born, that decision didn't feel so right anymore (or maybe it just felt even more wrong). It was such an overwhelming time and I had no idea how to handle it properly. Kenny and Lisa were just trying to do what was best for me and Callie.

LIFE WITHOUT CALLIE

The only thing I had to look forward to after my aunt and uncle took Callie home to Harlingen was that I would get to visit her soon. I missed her so much. I stayed in touch and I felt like I couldn't have asked for a better family for her. I was so fortunate to have been able to grow up around them and I was very appreciative that they believed in me and believed that I could do whatever I set my mind to. The problem was never the people I chose to adopt Callie. I couldn't have asked for better people if I had created a description of the perfect adoptive parents. No, the problem was the choice itself.

My uncle knew I was struggling with my decision. He sent me these two verses that really touched me. I put them on a sticky note on my desktop and read them every night:

"Greater love hath no man than this, that a man lay down his life for his friends." (John 15:13)

"Love is patient, love is kind. It does not envy, it does not boast, it is not proud. It is not rude, it is not self-seeking, it is not easily angered, it keeps no record of wrongs. Love does not delight in evil but rejoices with the truth. It always protects, always trusts, always hopes, always preserves." (1 Corinthians 13:4-7)

I know he was hoping those words would help me with my grief and pain, but that week at home without Callie was the most awful of my life. I waited for the constant crying, the wanting to die, the sense that I had made the wrong decision, to go away. But it didn't. All I could think was that I had made a mistake. I had to get Callie back.

As the days went by and those feelings didn't go away or get easier to deal with, I realized I had to do something. I called my uncle and aunt and told them that I wanted Callie back. I explained that I needed more time with her to see if I was capable of raising her on my own. If I didn't at least try, I would never know for sure if I had made the right choice. They were really understanding and told me to come get her. I didn't tell the MTV crew or anyone besides my mom that I was going. I just got on a plane and flew to Harlingen, determined to bring Callie back home with me.

BRINGING CALLIE BACK

In Harlingen I stayed with my stepdad. I didn't want it to be any more awkward for my aunt and uncle than it already was. When Kenny and Lisa gave Callie back to me, I could see for the first time how much they were hurting. They were supportive, but I realized this was hard on them, too. Looking back, I'm amazed at just how patient they were with me. In those first few days I was so freaked out that I might do something wrong. I kept calling Kenny to ask questions about changing her diaper and giving her bottles and he just kept reassuring me that I could do it.

Callie was still too young to get on a plane, so I stayed some extra time at my grandma's before heading back home to McKinney. By the time I got on the plane, the MTV producers had caught up with me, so I had the cameraman to keep me company on the flight.

I remember how hard it was, to go from knowing almost nothing about taking care of infants to suddenly being responsible for my own baby. Callie was two weeks old and I had so much to learn. I had her giant car seat, a huge suitcase, and a diaper bag that I had to haul through the airport. Waiting to board the plane, I realized it was time to feed her. I ran to buy her some good water to make her bottle. I even had to run to the bathroom to warm the water under a hot faucet because it was too cold. I was all over the place.

Meanwhile, I was constantly running to the restroom since it was only two weeks since she was born and I hadn't completely

healed. Frustrating and gross, right? So with all this and a flip camera in my face, Callie dirtied up her diaper right before we had to board. Poop everywhere. I had to laugh. I was just so relieved and elated to have her back with me.

Walking in the door with my daughter, back home in McKinney, I was completely overjoyed. I felt like I had my heart back. I could live again! Was I scared? Absolutely. The thought of being fully responsible for Callie was terrifying. But those two weeks without her had been so bleak that I knew nothing motherhood threw at me could be scarier than that.

HOME AGAIN

Emotionally, having Callie back with me was great. But the day-to-day challenge of taking care of a baby was very difficult. The first night was the hardest. At two weeks, Callie was waking up every two hours. It was exhausting, but I wasn't going to give up just because of a little sleep deprivation. I kept getting used to it and we quickly fell into a nighttime routine. Pretty soon she was drinking about three ounces of formula and sleeping three to four hours at night in between feedings.

For the first couple of days, I spent my time filling out college applications and taking care of Callie. Those were the most peaceful and content days of my life. I felt so blessed and fortunate to have her with me. But then real life came back. I had to get a job, because my mom wanted me to contribute to supporting Callie. I started working at the Walmart near my house, which meant I had to find someone to watch Callie while I wasn't home.

My mom agreed to watch her when she could, but she was pretty much working all the time. Justin's mom and my aunt Jen also offered to help with Callie, but I knew I couldn't rely on them forever. If I wanted to make this work I had to come up with a better plan. Day care was the most logical solution, but I hated the idea. How could I justify taking her back from Kenny and Lisa, just for her to end up being taken care of by strangers all day?

Meanwhile, with my every waking moment spent struggling to balance my time between Callie, working, and filling out college applications, everyday errands and even doctor's appointments became a treat. It felt like a luxury to get to go out for a little bit, even if it was just to go grocery shopping or to the OBGYN—I never thought I'd look forward to going there! Of course, I always loved coming home to my beautiful baby. That was the best. I always missed her when I went out, but it was a relief to have a few moments to myself.

So the blissful happiness of those first few days quickly faded. I worked, took care of Callie, and tried to focus on preparing for college. I constantly felt like I was treading water. I couldn't even put away Callie's clothes or move her in properly. She slept in a playpen in a guest room, which I later moved into with her. Her clothes just sat, folded in neat little piles, on the bed in my room. I wanted to buy her a crib and a changing table to get her more settled, but those things were expensive and my mom insisted that I wait until I was sure I was going to be able to keep her.

Plus, my mom wasn't cutting me any slack. She still expected the house to stay neat and for me to be able to take out the trash and clean up after myself and Callie. I was so tired and overwhelmed that I couldn't keep up with it all, so we started arguing again. Even when we went shopping, we ended up arguing because we were always in a rush to get back to relieve whoever was taking care of Callie. I could see the strain this was already putting on all of us.

I remember how hard it was keeping track of everything you needed for even the shortest outing: diaper bag, change of clothes, burp cloths, diapers, baby wipes, extra diapers, formula, pre-made bottles and powder for mixing bottles on the go. (I always ended up packing too much formula.)

Then it turned out that the powdered formula made Callie constipated and caused her a lot of pain, so I mostly had to use the pre-made kind. The tricky thing about not being able to mix formula from powder is that I had to make sure she ate right when we got to the restaurant or wherever we were because premade formula goes bad quickly if it isn't refigerated. The constipation was so bad that we almost had to use suppositories, which I really didn't want her to have to go through. Every time Callie felt pain, I felt like I had pain, too!

Another thing I remember about having a newborn is that, whether it's an explosive, poopy diaper or time for a feeding, you have to drop everything and take care of whatever your baby needs immediately. If she needed a bottle and we were out I would have to find some source of super hot water that I could hold a bottle under to warm it (I didn't like using a microwave because of hot spots in the bottle). If it was a poopy diaper, I had to find a changing room ASAP. The first day back I had a hard time changing her in the bathroom of an Italian restaurant—what a mess! But I laughed and found the accidents and messes humorous. It was far from easy, but I tried to take everything with a good attitude.

Forget about sleeping. Night after night, I would wake up to her cry that I knew meant she was hungry, run downstairs to the kitchen to prepare her bottle by warming it under the hot water faucet, then run back up to a now screaming baby that my mom usually got to before me. Then I'd feed her on the sofa while watching my shows I recorded on DVR especially for this occasion. She'd fall asleep in the middle of the bottle and I'd have to wake her up so she'd drink a little more. Sometimes we'd end up wasting the bottle. Then, the next morning I'd boil pacifiers and bottles and clean them and the process would start all over again.

I loved her so much and, as hard as it was, it was worth it. But I was stretched too thin and I began to feel like a failure, like I just didn't have what it took to be a single mom. Now, looking back, I think I was too hard on myself. For any new mom, that first month having your baby at home is overwhelming. You're sleep deprived, your hormones are raging through your body, and you have to take care of this other person who is completely dependent on you. On top of that, I had to deal with college applications, going to work, and proving to everyone (most of all myself) that this really was the best choice for Callie.

Probably for most moms in that first month, they just find a way to deal. They have no choice and they know the baby will be theirs forever. But I did have a choice and it was hanging over my head. Every time things were hard or I had to find someone to watch Callie, I couldn't help but think, *Is this the best way it could be? Is this the best choice for Callie?* Every time I wished I could go out instead of staying home with her, a voice in my head said, *There are people who want her who won't be unhappy if they can't go out. Wouldn't she be better off with them?*

Whenever I was depressed because I felt like all I did was take care of Callie and go to work, or I was bummed because I couldn't sleep late or go out and have fun, I felt guilty. I know now that this is something a lot of young new mothers feel. But most moms just have to figure it out. Their baby isn't going anywhere. I felt there was extra pressure on me that first month. I don't mean from Kenny and Lisa, because they were very supportive of my choice, even though I know it was extremely difficult for them. The pressure came from within. I was constantly comparing myself, and my struggle to parent, with the alternative that was being offered to Callie. Most new moms don't have to go through that.

Looking back, the whole thing is kind of a blur. I loved Callie so much. I loved being able to come home to her. I felt like someone depended on me and that I had a purpose. I learned so many new things about babies, about Callie, and about myself. I felt brave and strong. I'd barely even held a baby for more than a few seconds before and now I was taking care of my own daughter.

I sometimes wonder, if I had known then what I know now, would things have been different? Could I have figured it out? Or would I have been lulled into thinking I could do something I really couldn't? I guess I'll never know.

January

DECIDING

I was so exhausted and confused, my mom and I decided to reach out to Ashley, my original case worker from Gladney Center for Adoption. I hoped she would help me sort out my feelings.

Meeting with Ashley was great. She didn't try to push me in either direction, she just wanted to help me sort through it all so I could make the best choice possible for Callie. She said my choice was never going to feel one hundred percent right, either way. She told me that I was focusing on the weaknesses of each choice. This was stalling me, making me unable to either move forward as Callie's mom or commit to Kenny and Lisa adopting her. She encouraged me to focus on the strengths of each choice instead. It was the strengths that should guide my decision.

She reassured me that I should gain confidence from knowing

that I had managed to be a parent. If I chose to go through with the adoption, at least I would never have to wonder if I was capable of parenting. I had done it. With her help and encouragement, I was able to find the strength to call Kenny and Lisa.

When I talked to them I realized that they had been feeling almost as bad as I had felt during those first weeks after Callie was born because they loved her and missed her as much as I had. All this time I had thought that no one in my family could understand the grief I had experienced, but Kenny and Lisa had gone through a similar grieving process during the month that I had had her.

I have always felt truly blessed and thankful that I have such a wonderful family and that these awesome people allowed me to focus on my decision and take as much time as I needed. In the end, after all the agonizing back and forth, I finally made up my mind to stick to my original plan and let Kenny and Lisa adopt Callie. I still don't know if this decision was right. I do know that it was hard.

I couldn't face giving Callie back myself. My mom offered to do it for me and she drove Callie back down to Harlingen. The morning she left, I felt like my whole world had died. My friend Shelley came over and kept me company. While I was grateful to have her there, I felt dead and heartbroken. This was so much worse than any guy you've ever cried over. Watching my mom walk out the door with my baby, on her way to a new life, was the hardest, most heartbreaking thing I have ever experienced. I don't think anyone who hasn't had to give up their child could ever understand how I felt that day.

Yet, there were those who had never been through it who continued to criticize my decision. They said my reasons for adoption, such as wanting her to have stability and a more promising future, didn't matter. They argued that as her birth mother I could have given her more. I know I could have given her love, but I couldn't give her the kind of constant attention a baby needs. I just didn't have the luxury of being able to stay home with her. Usually it's just one stay-at-home parent, but in this case Kenny and Lisa both work from home. Callie was going to have a stay-at-home mom and a stay-at-home dad. That was pretty awesome to me. I ended up with the best situation anyone could have in an adoption.

I will always be in her life and she will always be able to know my story. She'll know that I tried. Of course, this time around I knew how hard it was going to be without her, but I finally felt I was ready to face that pain. I was stronger.

I'm not sure if I will ever be completely at peace with my decision. It happened. I made my choice. Now I have to live with it.

WITHOUT CALLIE

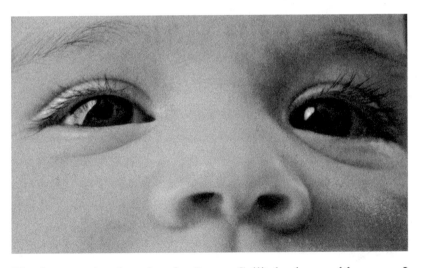

The first couple of weeks after I gave Callie back are a blur now. I did make short blog entries every day for the first couple of weeks. They are a real record of my state of mind:

Day 1

The way I figured I would feel. Sad and lonely. But it hasn't kicked in yet. I know it will, though. Blah. Sucky. The only thing is that I was much more prepared and I still stand by my decision.

Day 2

I feel angry. Still hasn't kicked in quite yet.

Day 3

Feel okay. Taking it day by day. Cried finally. But I try to just focus on other things.

Day 4

My days have been pretty lame. I have spent about 200 dollars in clothes, and I stay out until I'm exhausted so I can keep my mind off of things, then just fall asleep. I really haven't cried much and I feel really bad about that. But it's like hurting inside. I just think I've been so distracted that I don't. I go back to work tomorrow. Sucks!

Day 5

I want to cry, but it won't come out really. I'm doing alright, though. A LOT better than last time. Of course I'm always going to feel some sadness, but the happiness of knowing that she is taken care of

*will soon overcome the sadness and I can see her anytime I want to.
I'm glad I have all the support.*

*-ok, so the tears finally came, and a lot. I'm hurting, no doubt.
Who wouldn't be? Going out all the time only goes so far. Tonight I
stayed in, that's probably why. For anyone that says that I did this
out of selfishness, why would I put myself through this?*

Day 6
[Nothing]

Day 7
*I'm feeling a bit better, but still a little like...confused. Can't explain
it, but better, I suppose.*

Day 8
I've pretty much regressed.

*I slept back in Callie & my's old room
with the heater we used to use
and her blanket
dumb, I know
I go to bed crying*

I wake up crying

Nightmares

The only reason I am up right now is because I have to go to work at 4

and I don't have anyone here this time

I can't do this.

I'm probably just going through a bad stage

I'm done with blogging for a while

Day 14
WOAH. Day 14. It's been two weeks? It's really an up and down roller coaster. I feel so bipolar. I can't live without her. I need her here with me. I'll give up New York. I don't care.
It's not like it could happen anyway—New York. Probably not. Or getting her back. I'm so messed up for doing all this. I hate it. I hate the situation. I miss Justin and I have really barely any friends. I do need a new environment. But who cares? I just need MY baby.

Wow, that was all over the place and no one probably knows the half of it. Well, actually people don't...

Oh, today I took my ACTs. My mind was totally elsewhere. Math was what was going to save me. Math and writing. Writing was good. Math, I went super slow and didn't get to finish. Reading, eh—ok. Still slow. Science...I could NOT concentrate. I don't know ANYTHING. The questions were so much harder than the practice. My mind was so off. I kept thinking about Callie. I wanted to cry. I almost did. I marked every answer, well maybe 3/4s of it as C and G. It sucks. It really does. My SATs, I was too big to be comfortable in the desk because of being pregnant with Callie. My ACTs, I wished that I was too big to fit in that desk again with Callie that much closer to me. I'd honestly repeat the whole pregnancy over again. Back to day one when it all happened. I don't care. I miss her and I want to be close to her.

Day 16
I feel like somebody freaking died.

February

NYC

Just when I was at my lowest, something happened to take my mind off Callie for a little while. The MTV producers flew me out to New York to film some extra footage for my show. It was perfect timing because I could also take a tour of The New School.

At the time, I felt like one of the positive things that might come from giving Callie back to Kenny and Lisa was that I would be able to follow my dream. Back then, my dream was to move to New York and I was convinced that giving her up would have been pointless if I didn't take the big opportunities that came my way. If I went to college in New York and made something of my life, Callie would be proud of me when she grew up. I hoped that New York was where I belonged because it felt like there was nothing left for me in Texas.

I had an amazing trip. Shelley, my stepdad and I went all over

the city and took lots of pictures. I visited The New School, which MTV filmed for the close of my episode. We went to Times Square, SoHo, and the Brooklyn Bridge. We were total tourists. It was the first time I let myself have fun in what felt like forever. I was amazed by the city. New York was so big and loud and different. It wasn't like in the movies or photographs. I think everyone should go there at least once and see it for themselves.

While I was there I also got to meet some of the girls from other episodes of my season of *16 and Pregnant*. Seeing them was hard for me because they had all chosen to keep their babies. They had something to go home to. I felt like I had nothing. When it was time to go back home, I cried. I didn't want to leave. I felt like New York would distract me and maybe I wouldn't miss Callie so much. But in the back of my mind, I was worried that I just felt that way because it was a brand new place where I could start over. I guess I sensed even then that I couldn't run away from my problems.

BABIES EVERYWHERE

Going back to work was really hard. For me, working at Walmart wasn't the most exciting job in the world and unfortunately, in my case, I had too much time at work to think. I would constantly see adults with babies, carefree teenagers, pregnant teens, and teenagers that I knew had been pregnant and kept their babies. It made me so sad.

One day, I had a beautiful baby behind me, a baby at the register, a baby at the front of the store and another a few aisles away—all crying. You know how in movies when something happens and they focus on one sound and everything else is kind of blurry and indistinct in the background? Well, that's what that moment was like. Babies crying all around me. I felt psychotic. I fought back the tears as hard as I could. The lady I was checking out was probably like, *What is this girl's problem?*

I was a mess. I felt like I was on the verge of having a panic attack. I couldn't take it. I wanted to get the hell out of there and never come back. I wanted quiet. I didn't want to hear anything or listen to anyone. Crying babies were such a trigger for me. For one, I wanted to deal with a fussy, crying baby. I really did. And two, I never let Callie just sit there and cry. I didn't even let her fuss. If she was unhappy, I dropped whatever I was doing.

I felt like I was forgetting her face and how it felt to hold her, to bathe her, to take care of her and do all the little things she needed. I didn't think the way I felt was normal. Some people suggested I go on medication, but nothing could fill the void of my missing baby. No pill, no matter how strong, could fill the void. The thought of seeing her on breaks from school couldn't fill the void. Nothing could. Just like nothing could fill the void of my biological father not being around enough.

I didn't know if my thoughts were consuming me and making me incapable of moving forward. I didn't know what was holding me back. I just wanted her to have the best life she could have. So why was I in agony?

.

March-August

ACCEPTED

"On behalf of the Selection Committee, I am pleased to offer you admission to Eugene Lang College The New School for Liberal Arts for the class entering Fall 2010. Congratulations!"

In March I got accepted to The New School in New York City. I also got accepted to the University of North Texas, but that wasn't exciting. The New School was exciting. I had loved this school when I visited and I even got some financial aid money, so it was going to be affordable.

I started making plans to move to New York. I wanted to be excited for my future. I hoped that maybe not being in McKinney, not living in the house where I had held and washed and fed my baby, would allow me to finally make peace with my decision.

LIFE GOES ON...
KIND OF

In the meantime, I still came home every day to our empty house. It was especially hard to go downstairs at night to the kitchen. It reminded me of when I had been up making bottles for Callie. All I had left of her at home was a Chuck Taylor shoebox that contained her hospital hats and my copy of her footprints from the hospital. I slept with her blanket every night.

I wished I could relive that month that I had with Callie over and over again. I had been so happy. No matter where I went, I had something wonderful to come home to. Now it was beginning to feel like the past year hadn't happened, that I had never even had her.

I started thinking a lot about my biological father, Ray. When I was little and living in Harlingen, I used to see him sometimes.

Back then he was a minor league baseball player. I have this one memory of going to a baseball game to watch him play. He had told me that I could go home with him, but then after the game he just disappeared. I remember feeling so disappointed and betrayed.

Another time, he showed up at my mom and stepdad's house with a Nintendo 64. I don't remember much about that visit, but I do recall that my stepdad previously got very upset and told him to stop coming around if he was going to keep disappearing on me. The last time I saw him, he brought me to Burger King. My Mimi was babysitting me and my little sister, Mia. I remember he told me that he was going to go away for a while, probably to play baseball. But he never came back. I was six years old.

The fact that my biological father didn't seem to want me, the fact that I had chosen to allow someone else to raise Callie and she wasn't "mine" anymore, the fact that she might someday feel as abandoned by me as I do by my biological father, all those things began to eat away at me.

Two days before I moved to New York, I went to visit Callie. That was a really rough week. At the airport on my way back to Dallas, I realized I was sitting in the exact same seat that I had been in when I had brought her back home with me the previous December. My plane was even leaving from the same gate. Only this time I didn't have a cameraman along to talk to or a diaper to change.

I couldn't believe that almost one year had passed since I gave birth to her. It's kind of scary how everything seems to happen for a reason. Without Callie, I wouldn't have graduated as early as I did. I wouldn't have been moving to New York. I wouldn't have even cared much about college. I had wanted to go, but it wasn't something I was striving for.

Seeing Callie so happy and taken care of so well, helped me feel a little bit better about my decision. It took a lot to push aside my feelings and admit that I couldn't give my daughter what she deserved.

I know there are a lot of people out there who don't agree with the choice I made. I've been accused on my blog of being selfish. They say I could have done it. And you know what? They're right. Not about being selfish, but about being able to do it. I could have raised her myself, but it wouldn't have been the same. She wouldn't have had what she has now and she might have ended up making the same mistakes I made, the same mistakes my mother made.

I didn't cry when I said goodbye to Callie at the end of that visit, even though it hurt to know I wouldn't see her again for another four months. By then she would be a year old. It wasn't until later, sitting on the plane, that I felt the tears coming. I had to force them back, focusing on the music coming through my headphones and the faint sound of the plane's engine in the background. I didn't want to break down in public, all by myself. It's weird how you can feel no emotion in the middle of something very heartbreaking. Then the sadness can sneak up and overwhelm you—hours, days, even weeks later.

For instance, when my mom took Callie back to Kenny and Lisa the second time, I didn't really cry until almost a week later. Sometimes it just doesn't kick in right away. Then suddenly, out of nowhere, you get that feeling when the tears are gathering up behind your eyes and the wrong thought could trigger them.

I was moving on with a new chapter in my life. I was basically on my own, putting myself through college. If New York was going to be for me, I would know it. If it wasn't, I would find out and find a college closer to home. Either way, having Callie put my life into order. I didn't know what the future held for me, but I felt confident it held success. If not for me, then for Callie.

I had spent so much of the past year feeling sorry for myself. It was time to take a deep breath and let go of everything. Forgive everyone. Forgive my biological father for not being around enough. Forgive Justin for not being more supportive. Forgive my mom for whatever made me argue with her all the time. Forgive myself for giving Callie up.

September/October

HOMESICK

Once I got settled in New York, I started missing my family and Texas right away. Everything seemed wrong. I got a cold right away. Taco Bell didn't have a "79-89-99-cent" value menu. There was no Whataburger. Small details, I know, but these were things that were familiar to me and now everything was so different. The world was spinning and I had nothing to grab onto to help me keep my balance.

There were just so many people. Everywhere. Whenever I got on the subway there would be people jammed in all around me. When I was visiting New York, the subway felt like a novelty. Now that I was living there and it was my main mode of transportation, it felt crowded and uncomfortable, like everyone was crowding into my personal space. I missed my car and how it was almost like a home, the way you can stretch out in it and have all your important things with you. You can't do that on the subway.

What I did love about New York was the energy, the sense that lots of cool stuff was going on all the time. It was all there, just waiting for you to find it. New York is prettiest in late August, when it's about 7:00 A.M. and there aren't many people out. The weather is perfect and everything is so peaceful and calm.

IF I CAN MAKE IT THERE...

No matter how hard I tried, I couldn't concentrate on school. All I could do was sit and space out in class. I would think about Callie, Justin, my life back home. I would leave school and head back to my dorm with the intention of buckling down on some presentation that I had known about for weeks or doing some required reading for class. But then I would start thinking, *I mean, it's three-quarters done. That's okay, right? We have take-home tests in another class, so the reading isn't that necessary, right? Oh, and what song is that on TV? Why is my TV even on? I miss Callie so much...*

My mind was all over the place. I had thought getting myself away from all the things that reminded me of Callie was going to help, but instead it made me feel completely disconnected from my life.

But I was still trying to make a go of it in New York. I had really down days and I had really up days. I had depressing rainy days and beautiful sunny days. It was funny how I had wanted to call New York my home, but now that I was there I wanted to rep the Texas pride.

Moving to New York made me fall in love with Texas. I realized how much I loved driving. It made me appreciate my car and how good I had it. Texas is my home and it always will be. At least I could say I lived in New York. People say that if you can survive in New York, you can survive anywhere. I agree. It's an intense place.

For me, living in New York was kind of like getting from one place to another when it's bitter cold outside. You're shivering, your nose is super red and your body is numb, but you force yourself to adjust and keep walking. Sometimes it's for two blocks, sometimes ten. You can't wait to get to your next destination so you can just settle down for a little while and forget about that awful numb feeling…until you have to go back out and start all over again.

SHARING MY STORY

Whenever I was supposed to be working on some 1,500 or 5,000-word essay (that's twenty pages!), I would find myself posting on my blog instead, agonizing over my decision to give Callie up for adoption and whether or not I had done the right thing. Writing about and sharing my experience helped me process what I was going through, especially now that I was so far away from anyone who knew anything about me or my

story.

I felt that by sharing my life and feelings, I was doing a positive thing. At the same time, I wondered if I wasn't allowing myself to be a normal teenager. I couldn't stop, though. I was already so connected. I felt like my life was no longer just mine. Blogging and being on television made me feel both exposed and obligated. I felt I owed it to people, to those faceless blog readers and television viewers, to let them know how my life was going. When I signed my first real contract ever—to be on MTV—I had no idea how it would affect my life. It has been for the best, but sometimes it has felt like a big weight on my shoulders.

It was a weight I could feel when the trailer for my episode of *16 and Pregnant* started running on MTV. It was the same scene over and over: my mom and me crying on the worst night of my life, the night I signed the adoption papers. On the one hand I felt strongly that sharing my experience would help other young girls who were going through a similar experience to not feel so alone. On the other, it was painful to relive so publicly the only time in my life when I felt like I truly wanted to die. I hadn't seen any of the footage they had taken at that point, so I had no context for how they were going to portray my life. It was hard to have the most painful experience of my life broadcast for the world to see and judge.

NOT GETTING EASIER

My days in New York were so much harder to navigate than I had ever anticipated. One day, I was super late to class because I misplaced my key card to get into my dorm. I wouldn't have been so stressed about it, but some of the guards could be pretty mean. I left without it and thankfully a super nice guard was there when I got back.

Then I felt like my teacher was picking on me in class. He probably wasn't, but I was feeling ultra-touchy. I had gotten pretty good at hiding those feelings in person, though. Maybe. I ran out of class as fast I could, put in my earbuds, sucked up the tears and headed back to my dorm to try and find a place where I could cry alone.

I think the fact that it was always so crowded everywhere I went made me feel very edgy. It was impossible to really be alone in New

York. Back home, if I was feeling depressed, I'd take a long drive. I'd turn up the music and cry my eyes out. I could have my mini-breakdown in private and have a chance to pull myself together before having to face anyone again. In New York I couldn't do that, so I constantly felt like I was holding back a low-level breakdown.

At this point, even though deep down I knew I didn't belong in New York, I wasn't ready to commit to the idea of moving back to Texas. I wouldn't let myself. It was almost like I was trapped and that it was what I deserved. A big part of me felt that if I had stayed in Texas or if I decided to move back there, then that meant I should have been raising Callie myself.

You'd think that getting an update about Callie would have made me happy, like it did for Catelynn and Tyler, but it didn't. When I was sent photos of Callie it made being away all the more difficult. I asked for the updates, because of course I missed her and I desperately wanted to know every little detail about how she was growing and changing, but it hurt to see her face and not be able to be with her. But then I felt even more pain when I didn't get updates, so it was a lose-lose situation.

I had so much guilt weighing down on my heart. I didn't see how I was going to be able to leave Callie the next time I saw her. Being this far away from her for so long was awful.

NO PLACE LIKE HOME

The more time I spent in New York, the better I understood how I wanted to live my life. I wanted to live in a modern apartment and pay three times less rent for three times more space than an apartment in Manhattan.

I wanted to drive around with a couple of friends, blasting the music with the windows rolled down. I didn't want to refill my MetroCard and stand in a crowded subway car, body-to-body with sweaty strangers.

I wanted to stop at a red light with the heat on in the winter and the A/C in the summer. Not stand in the freezing cold, getting splashed with dirty water by cars in the winter, or sweating like I was in a sauna in the summer.

I didn't want to go to clubs, I wanted to go to a house and chill.

I wanted to feel safe at night, knowing nothing was going to happen to me.

I wanted to go to Walmart—not some organic food store—and buy double the food for half the price.

I wanted to go to the mall and buy clothes, without having to walk blocks and blocks to get there.

I wanted to drive through the country and get lost in the safety of my car. Not get lost walking in a sketchy part of town.

I wanted to go to a pizza buffet for four bucks, instead of paying four dollars for one slice. I wanted to go to a barbecue and have a burger, not go out for Chinese or Thai food.

I wanted to walk around in sweatpants on a lazy day—hair tied up, sunglasses on—and not feel like I was being judged.

I wanted to go back in time to January 25th, 2010—the day I gave Callie back for good.

So I finally made a decision. It was time to stop punishing myself. I weighed everything and decided to reapply to the University of North Texas. I missed home. I missed feeling comfortable in my own skin. As much as I loved Callie, I realized I had been making all my decisions for her. Now I was finally making a decision for myself.

November

NOVEMBER 11ᵀᴴ

I had finally come to terms with where my heart really belonged. To make it final, I didn't register for classes at The New School for the upcoming semester.

November 11th was the day that students were supposed to register for classes. It's very competitive and everyone gets up super early to sit at their computers to sign up for the classes they want. If you register too late, you won't get the classes you want. I woke up at 11:30 A.M. to a text from my mom that said she loved me and was proud of me.

I sat down to write my application essay to the University of Texas at Austin, another school close to home that I was considering transferring to. It felt like a sign. The topic was: *Write about somebody who has made an impact on your life.*

I remembered the feeling I had had when I finally made a decision regarding Callie. This time I felt so lifted making a decision for *me*. I had given living on my own in a big city a shot and learned it wasn't for me. It was time to stop running away from my problems and embrace what life had dealt me—head on. So it was final. I was leaving New York.

I think that maybe New York was just too liberal for me altogether. I never thought of myself as conservative, but I was kind of shocked by how people can lead any kind of lifestyle they want there. They are so open about some of the stuff they do, things that people would be way more discreet about in Texas. I guess I feel more comfortable in a place with more defined rules and values.

December

ONE FULL YEAR

December 2010 was a big month for me. My episode aired and I finally got to see what they had filmed. It was surreal reliving it like that, but I was happy with how MTV portrayed my story. There were some things that were left out that I thought would have helped to tell my story more fully (like when Justin signed the adoption papers, or my uncle and aunt cried at the hospital, or when I broke down before leaving the hospital), but overall I was happy with the footage they chose to include.

The other huge thing that happened that month was that Callie had her first birthday. One full year had passed since she was born and I had tried to keep her. So much had happened since then. I had learned so much about myself and had grown from all my experiences, both the positive and the negative ones.

I spent that Christmas with my stepdad's side of the family in Harlingen. I saw Callie as much as I could throughout this time. The previous Christmas, I had had Callie at home with me and seeing her again brought back some difficult memories. But it was amazing to see her more beautiful and ever. I couldn't believe how big and smart she was. She had a huge personality and a gigantic sense of humor.

I'm still doing my best to come to terms with my decision. I will always cry. I will always be lonely without her. Every time I leave her, I miss her little mischievous self, her laughter, her funny attitude, and her loving and innocent spirit. I am at peace knowing she is being taken care of so well by the family that I had wished was mine when I was younger. I still miss her every single day. I know that will never change. I just have to learn to deal with it better.

January

A NEW BEGINNING

January was an emotional rollercoaster. I was happy to be home, even though none of the issues that had been making me miserable were gone. The big difference was that I had learned that I couldn't change the past, but I could change how I dealt with all of it. I had definitely made the right decision to move back. It was better for me to be closer to Callie and to my family, and to the love and support I needed.

Moving back to Texas gave me a chance to start over, this time the right way and not by running away. My Mimi and Papa co-signed a lease for an apartment, so I was going to have a place of my own. It was a straight shot to the University of North Texas and the apartment was in the complex next to my stepdad's.

Not long after I moved back to Texas, and certainly when I least expected it, I met someone with whom I am able to have a stable and healthy relationship. He is someone who can bring me up from bad times and who is helping me deal with everything that I've been through. His name is Jordan and with his help I've learned that it's important for me to stay positive and healthy, as much for Callie's sake as for my own.

One night recently we went to a show by William Fitzsimmons, a singer/songwriter whose music was used in my episode. We went to the concert on the spur of the moment and Jordan and I decided to let the artist know we were coming via Twitter. The show was great, but the best part came when Fitzsimmons introduced a new song, one that he hadn't yet played on tour, by saying that it was, "For Ashley."

My heart stopped. He was dedicating a song to me! I knew which one it was going to be and I knew that it was going to mean a lot to me. It was "Find My Way Home," the song that played in my episode during Callie's birth. As he sang, I was taken back to that day: the best day of my life. In that moment, in a crowd of people, listening to a song that was personally dedicated to me, I felt wonderfully singled out. I stood completely still, thinking about my life—where I had been and where I was now.

Then Fitzsimmons played another amazing song, "Beautiful Girl." Where "Find My Way Home" makes me think of the day Callie was born, "Beautiful Girl" makes me think of the future and where my life is going. There's a line at the end, "May the weight of the world resign, you will get better," that gives me hope that I can make it through anything.

I had been through such a difficult experience at so young an age and it had changed my life forever. Where was I now? How far had I come? I wanted to just let go and let everything fall away. When I looked over at Jordan I could see that he knew exactly what was going through my mind. It made me realize I wasn't alone. Having the support of friends and family who care about me is what keeps me going.

Here is my new beginning. I have to accept my situation for what it is. Thinking about Callie or looking at photos of her still makes me so sad sometimes. But I have to turn my attitude around and tell myself, *You know what, Ashley? Callie was put here for a reason. She is a blessing to many and most importantly, she is a blessing to you.* Then I can gather my composure and go about my day.

Sometimes it still makes me sad that I didn't get to experience my last year of high school—even though I know that if I had been there I'd have been wanting to get out as soon as possible. Still, seeing everybody post their end-of-year pictures and say goodbye to all their friends really contributed to my sadness. But, then again, high school is overrated. I used to think everything in high school counted towards the real world. The truth is, it really doesn't.

I regret not waiting to have sex and I regret getting pregnant, but I don't regret my baby. I have to believe it will all work out for the best. Callie coming into this world is my greatest accomplishment. She is so beautiful that I know all of this happened for a reason. This is crazy, but the day she was conceived I was wearing an "I Love New York" T-shirt. Without her, I would have never been inspired to do anything.

When I get bitter or resentful, and I find myself holding onto my grief, I have to remind myself that I may have missed out on a few first milestones, but I have been blessed by God and my aunt and uncle with the privilege of being able to participate in Callie's life. I can tell that when she sees me, she knows me. At my last visit, she instantly lifted her arms up for me to pick her up. Moments like that are what keep me going.

Like I have said many times before throughout this long journey: If I could take away any type of pain or hurt that Callie might ever experience, I would. If this is my way to do it, then I'm going to do it. I believe that everything happens for a reason and that my experience has given me the strength and courage to know now that I can make it through anything life throws at me. I am uplifted and inspired by this beautiful, precious little girl.

I love you Callie, more than you will ever know. This is all for you. I miss you every moment I am not with you and I always will. You are my little angel. You are my everything.

THINK TWICE

One big message I want to get across is BE SMART. Once you are pregnant, you are pregnant. You are never just sort of pregnant. Use protection or, better yet, wait to have sex. Otherwise, one of four things will happen. You can miscarry, have an abortion, choose adoption, or grow up fast and become a parent. None of these are easy and all will profoundly impact the rest of your life.

Be smart. Be careful. Think twice, three, four, even five times before you do anything. Think about your potential child. Think about your loved ones. Think about yourself, while your life is still yours. Once you have a baby, that child will always be there—no matter what.

Compared to a lot of teens, I am really fortunate that my situation turned out the way it has. I have gained a lot from my experience, but I had to make the kind of painful grown up choices that no teen is ever prepared to make. I had to give up my baby. Nothing feels worse than that. Having her was the best and the worst thing that has ever happened to me.

ACKNOWLEDGEMENTS

First and foremost, God for blessing me with these opportunities and turning a potentially bad situation into something that I can deal with • My agent and new friend, Cheryl Pientka, and every single person I have worked with at MTV Productions and MTV Books • Elana Wertkin, for helping me believe in myself and start out this whole process, Allison Kagan and Rachel Elder, my three main ladies. I could have never gotten through the filming process without you • My roommates and other small group of New School friends that kept a hold on me in such a scary place for a whole semester. Y'all know who you are • My Mimi and Papa for always being there for me, not just as grandparents but as parents, every single day of my life without question no matter what • My mother, especially for raising me and putting up with my craziness and the grief I have given her for twenty years. Our happy and funny moments throughout this are the best memories, like when I ripped some maternity clothing at the store during filming. I really do love you with all of my heart and you are the best mom I could ever ask for • And yes. Andy • My crazy little sister, Mia. My dad for raising me as his own. And my Grandma Elizondo for opening up her house to me and Callie when I went to Harlingen to "get Callie back" • Uncle Kenny and aunt Lisa for being the most wonderful selfless people through this whole thing and my cousins Christian and Kastine. You basically saved my life • My aunt Jen and uncle James for always having an open ear and for opening up their home to me during this tough time when I had nowhere else to go and needed a place to just breathe. And to my little cousins Matthew and Alegra for keeping me sane while I was there • Jordan Baker for sticking with me during this time in my life and being a friend to me and Callie • Last, but definitely not least, my supporters who have been there with me before my show and after! Could never have made it through the criticism without you guys.

Note From MTV

Every single time you have sex there is a chance of pregnancy. The only 100% foolproof way to avoid pregnancy is to not have sex. If you are having sex, there are different methods of protection to choose from. To learn more about the method of protection that's right for you, visit:

www.itsyoursexlife.org

When you find out you are pregnant, you have three options to consider: to continue the pregnancy and keep the baby, to have the baby and choose an adoption plan, or to have an abortion. This is a big decision; take your time and talk with your partner, your family and other trusted advisers.

The National Council for Adoption can provide you with informational resources, as well as referrals to local adoption agencies.

National Council for Adoption:

www.ichooseadoption.org

Hotline: 1**-866-21-ADOPT (23678)**
Available 24 hours a day for information about adoption.

Also available by email at:

info@ichooseadoption.org